Introducing social studies

Jack Nobbs BSc (Econ) Dip Soc JP
Senior Tutor and Head of the Economics and Sociology Department,
Hewett Comprehensive School, Norwich

M

Macmillan Education

© Jack Nobbs 1979

All rights reserved. No part of this publication may be reproduced or transmitted, in any form or by any means, without permission.

First published 1979
Reprinted 1980

Published by
MACMILLAN EDUCATION LTD
Houndmills Basingstoke Hampshire RG21 2XS
and London
Associated companies in Delhi Dublin
Hong Kong Johannesburg Lagos Melbourne
New York Singapore and Tokyo

Filmset by Keyspools Ltd, Golborne, Lancs
Printed in Hong Kong

By the same author
Social Economics (McGraw Hill)
Modern Society (Allen & Unwin)

with Paul Ames
Daily Economics (McGraw Hill)

with Robert Hine and Margaret Flemming
Sociology (Macmillan Education)

with Robert Hine
Sociology Workbook (Macmillan Education)

with Marion Walton
Handbook on Objective Testing –
Civics (Methuen)

Contents

Preface		4
Unit 1	**You as a person**	6
Topic 1.1	You are unique	6
Topic 1.2	Which is the *real* you?	11
Topic 1.3	Why are you different?	15
Topic 1.4	What makes you human?	19
Topic 1.5	Making the most of yourself	23
Unit 2	**You and your family**	28
Topic 2.1	Your relations	28
Topic 2.2	Families	35
Topic 2.3	Family conflicts	38
Unit 3	**You and your friends**	43
Topic 3.1	Being a teenager	43
Topic 3.2	Friendships	47
Unit 4	**You and your education**	51
Topic 4.1	What should be taught?	51
Topic 4.2	Going to school	56
Topic 4.3	Communicating	62
Unit 5	**You and your local community**	70
Topic 5.1	Living in a community	70
Topic 5.2	Towns	79
Unit 6	**Living in our national community**	88
Topic 6.1	What is a national community?	88
Topic 6.2	Our government and the law	91
Topic 6.3	The national economy	98
Unit 7	**Living in the international community**	104
Topic 7.1	A divided world	104
Topic 7.2	Towards a united world	111

Preface

For many years schools have accepted the usefulness of teaching natural sciences to young teenagers, but only the more progressive have given much weight to the social sciences. It is hard to see why, when society is in such a mess and people find so much difficulty in resolving their conflicts.

This book provides an introduction to the social sciences. It starts with the individual as a person and the immediate world with which he or she is intimately involved: by studies of self, friends, family, school and community, a network of social relationships is investigated. The course is *concentric* and *conceptual* in nature.

1 *Concentric* because it tends to meet at a common centre, i.e. the individual pupil. (It is also divergent because it starts from the life of the pupil and then moves outward towards a discovery of a community, country and the world in which he or she lives.)
2 *Conceptual* because it leads to an elementary understanding of such concepts as heredity, environment, difference, conflict, cooperation, socialisation, role, division of labour, scarcity, causality, etc.

The book should be very useful to pupils taking courses which attempt to break down artificial subject barriers and often appear on the timetable as liberal studies or the humanities. It is not a watered-down sociology book, but includes elementary knowledge of many social sciences including sociology, economics, anthropology, psychology, politics and ethics. The author is grateful to Jean Hayhoe for her conscientious reading of the manuscript, for testing the suitability of the language for thirteen-year-olds on Fry's readability graph, and for her many helpful suggestions. The structure of the book also owes much to discussions with Richard

Whitburn of ILEA and Peter North of Avery Hill College of Education.

The book is based upon the proven technique of starting with knowledge related to the pupils' own experiences and then extending outwards to a deeper grasp of concepts of which they are as yet dimly aware. It offers a *living* course where young people learn through activity rather than as passive recipients of facts. Hence each topic concludes with a large number of things to do and think about.

Jack Nobbs
1978

UNIT 1
You as a person

These ornaments make this man from New Guinea distinctive but what is it that makes him unique?

TOPIC 1.1 **You are unique**

If you visited the island of New Guinea, off the north-east coast of Australia, it is possible you would see men who look like the one in the photograph, but you may not be able to pick our man out of a group of his countrymen. Others will adopt the same hairstyle and wear necklaces of shells. Yet this man is *unique*. There is no one exactly like him.

You also are unique. Each individual is unique. Each one of the millions of human beings on the earth is unique.

You may know other boys and girls who are very much like you. Sometimes people are so much alike that cases of mistaken identity occur. Occasionally a person is sent to prison because he is mistaken for somebody else. He is released when the real truth is discovered, but it is a bit late then to say, 'Sorry, but lots of people thought you looked like the real criminal.' He might have looked something like the criminal, but he was not exactly like him.

There is one way by which an individual's identity can be determined without any doubts whatsoever. That is by his or her fingerprints. No two people have exactly the same fingerprints.

Press your thumb on an inked pad. Now press your thumb, even more firmly this time, on to a piece of blotting paper. Compare the whirls of your thumbprint with those of your friends. If you have made good impressions each print will be clearly different.

Look at these prints. Only one of the 4000 million people in the world could have made them.

Thumb	Fingerprint

Fingerprint patterns

Have a really good look at the girls and boys in your class. They have different-sized mouths, noses and ears. How many have blue eyes and how many have brown? Are there any who cannot be grouped or classified easily by the colour of their eyes? Anyone with green or hazel eyes? How many different shades of hair colouring can you detect? What proportion are wearing spectacles? One quarter? One sixth? What proportions have black, brown, yellow or whitish skins? What other distinctive *differences* are there? Differences between people are many and natural.

Although your classmates have different weights, heights and skin colourings, they all look roughly the same. They form a group of young teenagers. There is no one three metres tall or weighing over 130 kilograms. But if one of you went to visit a tribe in New Guinea, you would stand out as being very different indeed. You would be regarded by the people there as being rather peculiar. If you look at the next photograph you should not have much trouble in picking out a lady called Felicitas who visited this group of Motilone Indians in the South American state of Colombia. To them, the colour of her hair and skin and her clothes must have seemed very strange.

Motilone Indians

YOU ARE UNIQUE 7

'But I AM wearing the school uniform, Mum.'

Groups of people take action to make members conform. Those who are unwilling to accept the norms of a particular society may be called eccentrics, delinquents or drop-outs. Can you think of ways you treat your friends to make them conform?

Have you heard of Timothy Winters? This is a funny example but young people can be very unkind to boys like him.

> Timothy Winters comes to school
> With eyes as wide as a football pool,
> Ears like bombs and teeth like splinters;
> A blitz of a boy is Timothy Winters.
>
> His belly is white, his neck is dark
> And his hair is an exclamation mark
> His clothes are enough to scare a crow
> And through his britches the blue winds blow.
>
> CHARLES CAUSLEY

You and your schoolfriends have a similar appearance to each other because you *conform* – that is, you all look and behave in a similar way. The behaviour of the Motilone Indians includes customs such as carrying spears, painting dark blotches under their eyes and wearing long robes. You and your friends have special types of behaviour – can you think what they are? When people in a group act in a similar way we say that they adopt *group norms*.

If someone goes against the norms of the group then he is likely to be isolated or left out because he is thought to be unusual or different. The lady in the photograph was in great danger because it is the custom of Motilone Indians to attack strangers who try to photograph them. When people from different groups meet, *conflict* may arise because of a lack of understanding (see page 9). This conflict can be lessened if people get together and accept each other's customs. But it is often difficult to reach agreement.

Things to do and think about

1 What things about a boy or a girl would tend to make you regard them as strange? Write a short passage beginning with the words, *either*:
   (a) 'Strange people frighten me.'
   or:
   (b) 'We need individualists who stand out against the crowd.'
2 Look again at your answer to question 1 and try to work out why you think the way you do. Discuss your reasons with your friends.
3 Collect newspaper cuttings about individuals who fail to conform to the behaviour of the majority.
4 Remember the man in the photograph who wore a stick through his nose? Find examples of similar habits which appear peculiar to us but which are accepted as normal in other parts of the world.
5 Find examples of customs which we take for granted and which other people, such as the Motilone Indians, might think

Anti-Hunt Demonstrations 5 Arrested

5 MEMBERS of the Aston branch of the Campaign for the Abolition of Blood Sports were arrested when they tried to force a senior member of the Corbett Hunt to dismount. According to Mr George Wickens a small group of the demonstrators surrounded two of the youngest hunt riders and tried to dissuade them from taking part. When Mr Wickens rode over to see what was happening, the group turned on him making his horse rear. They then seized the reins and attempted to pull Mr Wi... from ... orse 'This
 ... highly ...

Demolition workers take off the wrong roof

RESIDENTS of Longacre Road, Camden, were horrified as they saw the demolition workers start to take the tiles from Number 37, the fourth house in a terrace of six. Numbers 31, 33, 35 were scheduled to come down as part of the new road scheme, but Number 37 had been reprieved – at least till last Monday. Mrs Sullivan, who lives across the road to the house, saw one of the demolition workers on the ...of and asked what he was doing there, as the house

Anger at the Longacre Road plan

CAMDEN'S latest plan to speed traffic through the borough again has controversy between the parties involved. Longacre Road is going to be widened, to ease some of the congestion in Bagholt Road. There is also to be a new road linking Longacre Road to Moor Park Close, which will mean the demolition of several houses. Residents of Longacre Road protested angrily outside the town hall while the meeting w.s in progress. Later ... inv..led the ch..ber and
 ...

Gypsies threaten to camp on old quarry site

6 GYPSY families were tonight threatening to camp on the Laurelston Quarry site, at present used as a storage depot by Cumberland road works department. The site provided at Hill Farm Lane is not big enough to hold the families, and is already occupied by 4 ... families. The road ...s depa...t want

Neurology Unit should be returned to us claims hospital

THE bitter argument between the two London teaching hospitals today reached a head when the senior consultant of the unit stated that he would ...ht ...st the d...on, t..en on T...rs...t
 ...d ...

YOU ARE UNIQUE 9

CASE AGAINST HAIN WOULD NOT CONVICT A CAT, SAYS QC

HAIN: so far the identity score is four Yesses and 11 Noes or Don't-knows

HAIN'S GLASSES REMOVED FOR BOY TO EXAMINE

funny, e.g. eating fish and chips, wearing scarves at a football match, wearing eye make-up.

6 In 1975, a young politician called Peter Hain was accused of robbing a bank. He was found not guilty on the grounds of mistaken identity, but it made people think very carefully about how reliable identification parades are. Imagine you are a police inspector. What details of an accused person would you require if you wanted to organise an identification parade?

7 Take fingerprints of members of your class. Which two people have:
(a) similar prints,
(b) very different prints?
Have they any other similarities or differences?

8 Without carrying out a detailed investigation, choose the statement you think is most likely to be correct:
(a) Most people in the class have brown eyes.
(b) Most people in the class have blue eyes.

The one you have selected is a *hypothesis*. This means it is a statement which can be used as a basis for reasoning, but it does not mean that it is true. When a hypothesis is put to the test it may be shown to be either true or false. So let us now test these hypotheses to see which one is true and which one is false. If more than half of your classmates have brown eyes then (a) is right; if more than half have blue eyes then (b) is right. Now suppose a large number have green eyes, so that less than 50 per cent have brown eyes and less than 50 per cent have blue eyes. Alter your original theory and produce an accurate conclusion.

You have now made a hypothesis, tested and modified your theory, and come to a conclusion. That is a social science investigation. All the information we have about society is gained in a similar way.

9 What is meant by 'sending people to Coventry'? Where did the expression originate? Why might a group of children send a person to Coventry?

10 The French sometimes call childhood *L'age sans merci*; this means the age without pity. Why is a gang of children often very unkind to someone who seems somewhat different from the rest? Without mentioning names, describe some examples of cases known to you.

TOPIC 1.2 **Which is the *real* you?**

As we grow up we have fantasies about who we would like to be. It may be a famous footballer, or pop singer or even the Queen.

On occasions we all like to imagine that we are famous:

Tibbut, standing on the centre circle, with his hands down his shorts, winked at his left winger and waited for Mr Sugden to approach.

'Who are you today, sir, Liverpool?'

'Rubbish, lad! Don't you know your club colours yet?'

'Liverpool are red, aren't they, sir?'

'Yes, but they're all red, shirts, shorts and stockings. These are Manchester United's colours.'

'Course they are, sir, I forgot. What position are you playing?'

Mr Sugden turned his back on him to show him the number 9.

'Bobby Charlton. I thought you were usually Denis Law when you were Manchester United.'

'It's too cold to play as a striker today. I'm scheming this morning, all over the field like Charlton.'

BARRY HINES, *A Kestrel for a Knave*

When you were very young, you played lots of make-believe games. Some of them may well have provided useful training for what you are going to do when you are grown up. You

What kind of fantasies do you have?

WHICH IS THE *REAL* YOU? 11

probably shared your fantasies with your parents and they played along with your imaginary games. As you grew up your make-believe gave way to more realistic thoughts but even as grown-ups you may have ideals about what you want to achieve.

What is an optimist? Someone once said, 'An optimist is a man who sees a light which isn't there, whereas the pessimist comes and blows it out.' The optimist in the pub looks upon his glass as half full, but the pessimist complains that his glass is half empty!

Even when you are grown up you continue to play different parts or *roles*. This is very much a part of your life. You are a member of several groups of people. At school you are a pupil; at home you are a son or daughter, brother or sister; to your neighbours you are the boy or girl next door; to the people in the village, town or city where you live you are a fellow citizen; and to people in other countries you are a foreigner. These are just some of the roles you play in life.

Although you are really always the same person, you take on these different roles at different times. Often you can play more than one role at the same time. Sometimes when this happens you may feel what social scientists call *role conflict*. Imagine that mother wants you to babysit and your boyfriend (or girlfriend) wants you to go to the disco. You feel a conflict because you

Different roles you can be expected to play

probably want to play the role of friend, but you feel you ought to do what your mother wants and play the role of son or daughter!

Do you talk to your teacher differently from the way you talk to your friends? Do you act differently at home depending on which members of the family are there? We shall examine later how we behave differently when we are part of a group of people.

What is the attitude of the boy in the picture to the policeman? Can you imagine the same boy in a few years' time becoming a football hooligan who smashes up a train and commits acts of vandalism? Human feelings are very complicated and are often only faintly understood by the individual concerned. In this book we shall learn much more about ourselves. We will see how we are continually being changed by our surroundings. This change is known as *modification*.

Football hooligans sail home from jail

By
Robert Francomb

SIX Manchester United supporters branded as hooligans by a Belgian court sailed home last night protesting about the way they had been treated during five weeks in prison.

'We were handled like animals,' said 18-year-old Vincent Peet. 'We were kept in solitary confinement and the food was uneatable.'

Behind them in Belgium they left judges, lawyers and people-in-the-street who were appalled at the way the young Britons had treated Belgian property.

'We will not tolerate people who destroy property for wanton pleasure' said the prosecution at the Bruges courtroom where the fans were given suspended prison sentences of three months, fines of £30 each, and ordered to pay £350 damages between them.

The prosecutor, M Jean Marie Berkvens went on: 'The image of the British gentlemen along the Belgian coast has given way to one of truculent and drunken youths throwing cobblestones and wielding sticks.

He demanded a severe sentence as a deterrent 'because people abroad are watching the outcome of this trial.'

And though the judge decided on three months' imprisonment all round he suspended all of the sentence not covered by the five weeks they had spent in jail on remand.

The 'rowdies' were taken to court from prison in handcuffs.

After the hearing the manacles came off and on went United scarves and Tam O'Shanters.

The six went for a drink or two or three and then caught a boat for Dover.

As they came ashore last night Peter Brunt, aged 23, of Camberley, Surrey, said: 'We were treated terribly in prison. We were in solitary confinement for over 23 hours a day.

Peter added: 'Whether I pay the fine depends on whether I go back to Belgium.'

Vincent Peet, who lives in Manor Way, Colindale, London said: 'They say I wrecked two cars but how could I have done that on my own?'

Robert Mahoney (18), of Whitefield, near Manchester, has been forbidden by his father from going to any more football matches for the time being.

Things to do and think about

1. A person who likes to pretend that he is Hitler might be described as power-mad. Suggest reasons why people might like to imagine that they are:
   (a) the Pope
   (b) a soccer star
   (c) a weightlifter
   (d) a fashion model
   (e) a drummer in a successful pop group
   (f) a missionary
   (g) a brain surgeon
   (h) the Queen
   (i) a ballet dancer
   (j) an undertaker.
2. Pretend that you are one of the people mentioned above and relate an amusing happening.
3. Think of some situations in which you would feel role conflict. Discuss among yourselves how you would resolve the conflict.
4. Try to put yourself 'in the shoes' of *either*:
   (a) a white child in a class made up mostly of coloured children
   or:
   (b) a black child in a class of whites.
   Describe your innermost feelings.
5. Suggest five words you associate with the role of a:
   (a) toddler   (c) mother
   (b) teenager   (d) grandfather.
6. Draw a strip cartoon illustrating the various roles of a typical man or woman. Some ideas are given below to help you.
7. In what ways could you help your mother to fulfil the roles of a woman out at work and a mother of a family?
8. In what ways do your teachers' lives resemble your own? For example:
   (a) which teachers like pop music?
   (b) which ones support your local football team?

14 INTRODUCING SOCIAL STUDIES

Physical resemblance to our parents is controlled by genes passed on in our parents' chromosomes

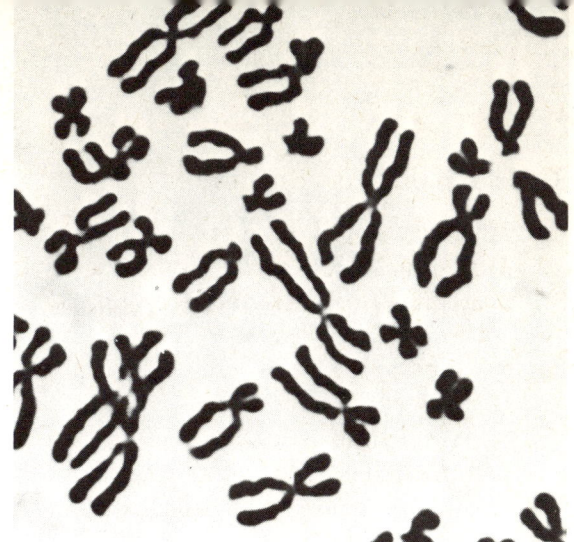

Some human chromosomes magnified many thousand times

TOPIC 1.3 Why are you different?

The boy in the photograph is unique. Yet he looks similar to his mother and father. Which parent do you think he resembles more? Look at the shape of the mouth and eyes.

There are two ways in which children are like their parents. One is by *heredity*: they inherit physical features from their parents. The other is because they have learned behaviour from them.

An individual receives twenty-three chromosomes (as they are called biologically) from each parent. These forty-six chromosomes are of great importance because they determine everything about the physical characteristics of the baby. Our knowledge of the working of heredity is incomplete and we do not know how much of our behaviour is inherited, but we do know that the colour of our hair, eyes and skin, our body type and even the shapes of the lobes of our ears are influenced by these curious thread-like structures called chromosomes.

These chromosomes are passed on as part of the reproductive process. The father passes on his twenty-three chromosomes by way of a sperm. The mother passes on her twenty-three chromosomes by means of an egg but, although the child grows inside her while she is pregnant, she has no more influence over the child's heredity than the father.

Do you look more like your mother or your father? Although you will probably have little doubt about which parent you mainly take after, it is quite possible that your brother or sister will more closely resemble your other parent. Do you think that the girl in the photograph below is very much like her

Another example of heredity – compare this girl and her mother with the family above

WHY ARE YOU DIFFERENT? 15

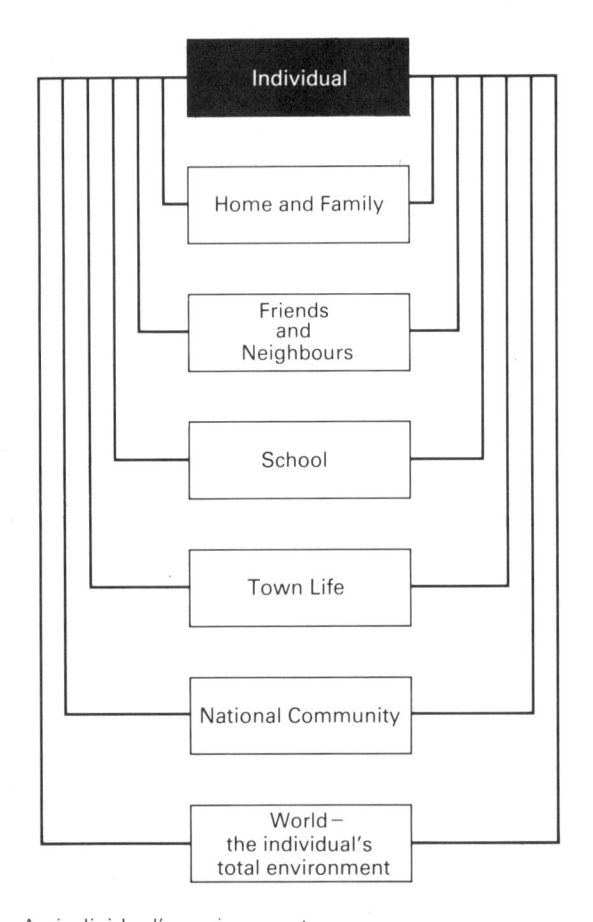

mother? Yet she is still a separate individual. She has her own feelings, her own thoughts and her own personality.

We saw above that, apart from heredity, the other influence which helps to determine what sort of person you are is the behaviour you learn from your parents; and, we should add, not only your parents but the rest of your world – your *environment* or your surroundings. The sort of environment in which you are brought up is a question of chance. You may be born into a rich home, or a poor one; your parents may spend a lot of time with you, or they may leave you very much to yourself. You may live in the town or in the country, and you may have many brothers and sisters, or be an only child. All of these factors form your environment and make you what you are. Can you think of any others?

The baby in the photograph is fortunate. She is kept spotlessly clean and enjoys being out in the open air with her toys. Her parents love her and spend a lot of time playing with her and helping her to learn and develop. No wonder she looks happy.

An individual's environment

'No, I haven't changed my mind about running away to sea. My shoelace is undone.'

16 INTRODUCING SOCIAL STUDIES

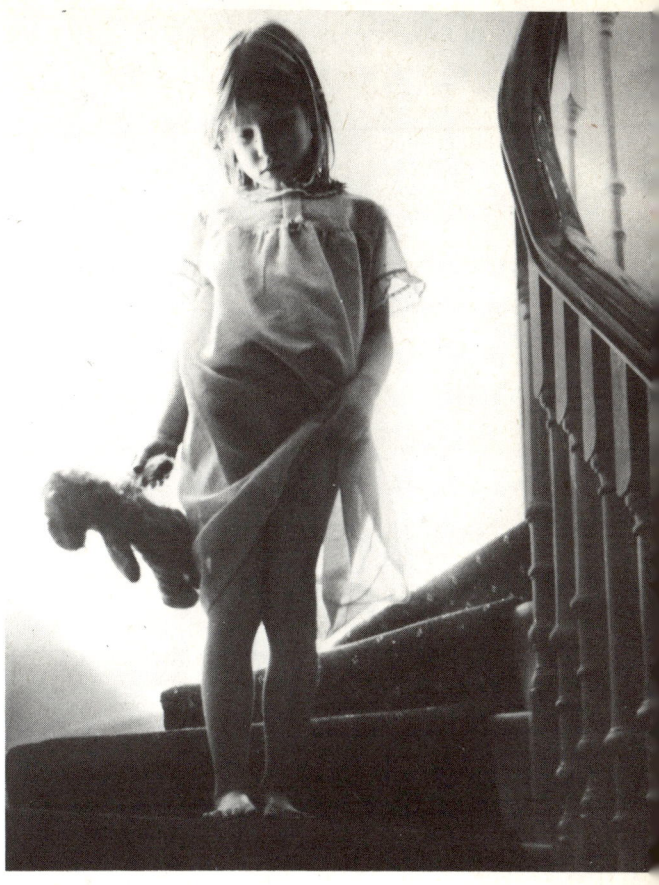

Look at these two children – how have they been neglected?

The little boy in this photograph is not so lucky. His father and mother have little time for him. He has no one to wipe his nose. His clothes are in tatters and no one really cares. His parents do not help and guide him while he is growing up. He will have to learn about life the hard way.

Social scientists study the way people live in groups. It is thought by sociologists and psychologists that the first few years of a person's life have the greatest influence upon the way his character develops. We have seen how some characteristics are inherited, and some are learned. There are usually many causes which have contributed to a person's happy or unhappy disposition. Social scientists are interested in *causality* or the study of causes.

Most parents are fond of their children and want them to have the chance of developing into the best people they can possibly be. But because of differences in parents' income, housing conditions, and the quality of education in different schools, children do not have equal opportunities.

This girl's mother and father have gone out and left her without a babysitter. She looks unhappy because she is frightened of being alone at night.

Children learn more from the example of

WHY ARE YOU DIFFERENT? 17

How many cigarettes a day does your child smoke?

When a child breathes air filled with cigarette smoke it can be as bad as if he actually smoked the cigarette himself. Don't smoke when there are children present.

The Health Education Council

parents than by the words they speak. When you are a parent will you smoke in front of your children? We know that over 30 000 people each year die of lung cancer and that the great majority of these are very heavy smokers. Nobody would offer a small child a cigarette yet many parents encourage their children to smoke by smoking in front of them.

An individual is even influenced by the environment of the mother's womb before birth. If a mother smokes during pregnancy her child, at the age of seven years, is likely to be about one centimetre shorter than the average child of that age.

As we have seen, people are far from equal because they have inherited different characteristics and live in different environments. But many people feel that society should break down inequalities as much as possible so that everybody can have equal opportunities. According to the United Nations Universal Declaration of Human Rights, each person is born free and equal in dignity and rights.

Part of the Universal Declaration of Human Rights

18 INTRODUCING SOCIAL STUDIES

The Declaration sets out the ideal of members of the human family (family here is in the sense of all the people in the world, i.e. the human family) acting towards each other in a spirit of brotherhood. Most of us wish that people always behaved kindly and that each individual enjoyed complete freedom, justice and peace. In a perfect world this might be so but in the real world there is too much conflict of interests for this to happen.

As long as there are inequalities there will be conflict. Conflict is not always a bad thing, but a lot of good can arise from a peaceful solution to differences of opinion. Despite the inequalities in the world, we can try to sort out our problems on the basis of the Declaration of Human Rights.

Can you see any parallels between conflict within the members of a family or among friends, and that on a world scale between different countries?

Things to do and think about

1. We have learnt that the sort of people we are depends a lot upon chromosomes which transmit features we inherit. Chromosome numbers are constant for each species. Rearrange the following to make correct pairings:

species	chromosomes
bee	46
cat	48
fly	40
man	16
mouse	8
potato	38

    You will need a copy of *Pears Cyclopaedia*, or a good biology book, to do this. Can you find out any medical disorders which are connected with incorrect chromosome patterns? For example, a mongol child has an extra chromosome.

2. What features of your environment have influenced you most:
    (a) at home
    (b) at school
    (c) in your neighbourhood?

3. Relate an account of a person born in poor surroundings who overcame his or her disadvantage and achieved success and fame.

4. Name a person who has decided to drop out of society. Explain why he or she made this decision.

5. Write out one of the main points in The Universal Declaration of Human Rights and explain why you think it has been included.

6. Choose *one* of the following parental statements and say why you support it.
    (a) 'I intend to make sacrifices to give my children the best possible opportunities in life.'
    (b) 'I had to rough it so I believe my children ought to rough it too.'
    Are there any other possible attitudes?

7. What does a child learn in the first five years of life? Why are those things so important for the child's development?

8. Make a list of types of people:
    (a) who are rejected by others
    (b) who reject others.

TOPIC 1.4 What makes you human?

Differences

Hundreds of different fish in the sea,
Thousands of different leaves on a tree,
Different creatures, different birds,
Different books and different words.
Different people with different ways,
Millions of minutes and countless days.
I'm not like you and you're not like me
But we're part of the human family.

What are the main differences between human beings and other creatures of the animal kingdom? We share many of the same behaviour patterns.

Both humans and animals reproduce their own species, and most care for their young. Both show *instincts* of aggression, fear, hunger, and most live in social groups. This kind of behaviour is sometimes called instinctive.

Nobody really knows how much instinctive behaviour is really learned after birth. A baby sucks at the breast. The sucking action is probably instinctive. Soon the baby displays curiosity and seeks to find out more about the world. When frightened it shows fear, and when amused it laughs. But a lot of this behaviour may have been learned from the mother or other people. For example, a baby can learn how to be frightened and how to laugh from its parents' reactions – even from very early in its life. One of the greatest forces in both animals and humans is the struggle to survive, and offspring probably learn from the parents how to do it.

As a human being you do other things as well. You think things out. You are part of *homo sapiens*: *homo* means 'mankind' and *sapiens* means 'thinking'. It is this thinking ability which makes human beings different from animals. From this comes the development of words and languages, the use of numbers, the designing of complicated tools and machines, and the passing of judgement upon acts of behaviour so we say that a good act is 'human' (or humane), while a bad act is considered inhuman or unworthy of a human being.

> Man is the only animal that laughs and weeps; for he is the only animal that is struck with the difference between what things are and what things ought to be.
> WILLIAM HAZLITT

It has taken thousands of years for modern men and women to develop. In recent years Richard Leakey has discovered (in the African country of Kenya) a fragmented skull which seems to prove that human beings existed over 2 500 000 years ago. Leakey's human was quite a big-brained person who walked upright and made tools of stone. The first appearance of a modern human being, *homo sapiens*, is not known exactly but is thought to have been less than 500 000 years ago.

The long process, by which early man became modern man, is known as *evolution*. In the nineteenth century Charles Darwin put forward the theory that the evolution of modern human beings has occurred because the fittest have survived and passed on to their descendants the ability to survive. The characteristics which enabled man to survive in his environment were passed on through the chromosomes. Those less suited to the environment died and their characteristics died with them. This is called evolution by *natural selection*. You will want to discuss this concept further, but it must be pointed out that the theory is not completely accepted by scientists.

Human beings are what they are because of their heredity, environment, experiences, thought-processes and emotions.

Can you control your emotions? We all have to handle our feelings of fear and amusement, of happiness and sadness. We learn how we should do this from the culture in which we live. For example, in some societies people laugh at funerals, whereas we show sadness. We learn to direct our emotions in the way society expects of us. We learn from *experiences* so that the same mistake is not made over and over again. Can you think of an example of one of your pets learning from experience?

As human beings we all control our real feelings at one time or another. A little child asks you what you think of the picture she has

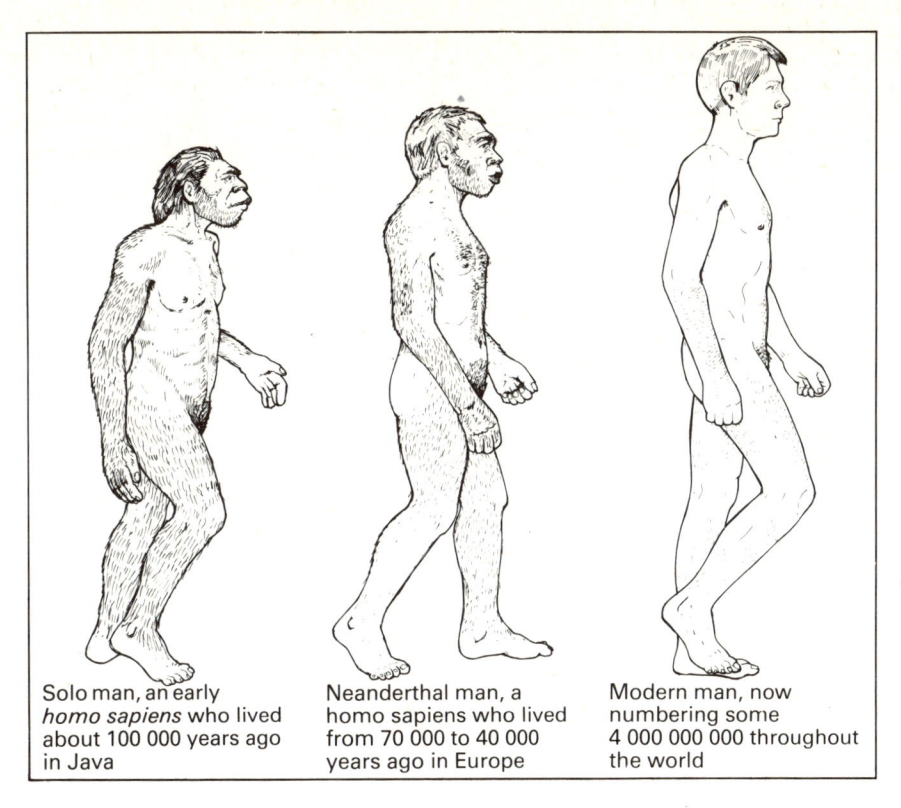

Solo man, an early *homo sapiens* who lived about 100 000 years ago in Java

Neanderthal man, a homo sapiens who lived from 70 000 to 40 000 years ago in Europe

Modern man, now numbering some 4 000 000 000 throughout the world

The evolution of man

drawn. You may think it is a dreadful picture. The sky is yellow, the ground is purple and the people look like dinosaurs. You pretend it is lovely because you don't want to upset her. Our behaviour is influenced by our relationships with other human beings.

Also as a person you have to make decisions continuously about values. You have to make judgements and decisions whether you like it or not. You cannot act like the sailor in A. A. Milne's poem:

The old sailor

There was once an old sailor my grandfather knew
Who had so many things which he wanted to do
That, whenever he thought it was time to begin,
He couldn't because of the state he was in.

He was shipwrecked, and lived on an island for weeks,
And he wanted a hat, and he wanted some breeks;
And he wanted some nets, or a line and some hooks,
For the turtles and things which you read of in books.

And, thinking of this, he remembered a thing
Which he wanted (for water) and that was a spring;
And he thought that to talk to he'd look for, and keep
(If he found it) a goat, or some chickens and sheep.

Then, because of the weather, he wanted a hut
With a door (to come in by) which opened and shut
(With a jerk, which was useful if snakes were about),
And a very strong lock to keep savages out.

WHAT MAKES YOU HUMAN? 21

He began on the fish-hooks, and when he'd begun
He decided he couldn't because of the sun.
So he knew what he ought to begin with, and that
Was to find, or to make, a large sun-stopping hat.

He was making the hat with some leaves from a tree,
When he thought, 'I'm as hot as a body can be,
And I've nothing to take for my terrible thirst;
So I'll look for a spring, and I'll look for it *first*.'

Then he thought as he started, 'Oh, dear and oh, dear!
I'll be lonely tomorrow with nobody here!'
So he made in his note-book a couple of notes:
'*I must first find some chickens*' and '*No, I mean goats.*'

He had just seen a goat (which he knew by the shape)
When he thought 'But I must have a boat for escape.
But a boat means a sail, which means needles and thread;
So I'd better sit down and make needles instead.'

He began on a needle, but thought as he worked,
That, if this was an island where savages lurked,
Sitting safe in his hut he'd have nothing to fear,
Whereas now they might suddenly breathe in his ear!

So he thought of his hut . . . and he thought of his boat,
And his hat and his breeks, and his chickens and goat,
And the hooks (for his food) and the spring (for his thirst) . . .
But he *never* could think which he ought to do first.

And so in the end he did nothing at all,
But basked on the shingle wrapped up in a shawl.
And I think it was dreadful the way he behaved –
He did nothing but basking until he was saved!

It is often very difficult to make these decisions. Will you always act generously? Would you lend money to a person who was drunk and acting in a way which would bring him into trouble with the police? A man visits his dying wife in hospital, but she does not know their son has been killed that very day in a motor cycle accident. He assures her the boy is all right. Has he done the right thing? A human being is the highest form of life; life for him is rich and varied, but it is also complex and difficult. He has a sense of *values* or socially accepted behaviour and ideals. Values differ between groups of people.

Things to do and think about

1. Rearrange the following into correct pairings, e.g. fight and anger:

behaviour	*emotion*
fight	fear
escape	tenderness
curiosity	wonder
ownership	anger
parenthood	creativeness
repulsion	acquisitiveness
construction	pride
self-assertion	amusement
laughter	disgust

   Now compare your list with your neighbour's.
2. Read an account of the work of Ivan Pavlov in an encyclopedia. Write a brief account of his experiments in feeding his dog. How much of our own behaviour do you think results from some kind of conditioning?
3. Write a case to support one of the following statements. Give reasons for your opinion.
   (a) We all come from monkeys.
   (b) Man was created after God's own image.

Are they alternatives or could both be true?
4. Draw a settlement which might have been inhabited by Neanderthal man. Remember his need for shelter, food, tools, clothes and water.
5. If you were stranded on a desert island by yourself, what things would you miss most?
6. List some ways in which you think relationships with parents, brothers, sisters and friends have helped you to learn to live in your environment. Would you be the same person if you had been born into a different family?
7. What feelings do people experience after they have had a terrible row?
8. Tell a story to illustrate the saying 'Bravery is being scared stiff and still doing what you have to do.'
9. What *biological drives* enable us to survive? (For example, we eat when we are hungry and sleep when we are tired.)

TOPIC 1.5 Making the most of yourself

We are all different but each of us has his own best to offer.

The Queen's Christmas Message, 1975

The British nation is made up of many different peoples, who for centuries have been coming to these islands. The strength of the nation has been the successful blending together of so many different people: Celts, Picts, Scots, Ancient Britons, Romans, Anglo-Saxons, Danes, Norman-French and immigrants from many other lands. We are descended from a mixture of races (see page 24).

This process is still going on. Since the Second World War, many more peoples have been coming to the British Isles: Poles, Lithuanians, Czechs, Indians, Pakistanis, West Indians, Hungarians to name a few. Can you think of others?

The richness of the life of your school community depends upon the working together of very different people. We differ in sex, build, intelligence, interests, colour and background. Some come from happy families where life is fulfilling; others are from homes where there are problems. Some of your friends at school may come from Catholic homes, some from Protestant homes, Jewish homes, Muslim homes, Hindu homes or homes with no religion at all. They come from different neighbourhoods: they live in terraced houses, high-rise flats, or on housing estates, in detached or semi-detached dwellings and bungalows. In what ways has the sort of dwelling you live in influenced your life?

There are some strong feelings about regional differences in the British Isles. You have probably seen on the television news and read in the papers that it has finally been decided to set up separate parliaments for the Welsh and the Scots. The Cornish people also claim they are very different from people in other parts of Britain. Some of the Welsh use their own language which they feel is part of their heritage and which they want their children to learn. But there are also less obvious regional differences. For example, many people in the north of England, 'northerners', also feel they have special social and economic problems in the same way that the Scots and Welsh do, and consider that they should be treated as a separate region as well.

The success of a school depends upon the blending together of different people who make up the whole community. 'Each has his own best to offer.' An important part of education is learning to live with different people. Some people blame the system or the institution when things go wrong. Institutions are made up of people like you and me and all the others. Society is made up of all the people in it.

Men have always had visions of how people

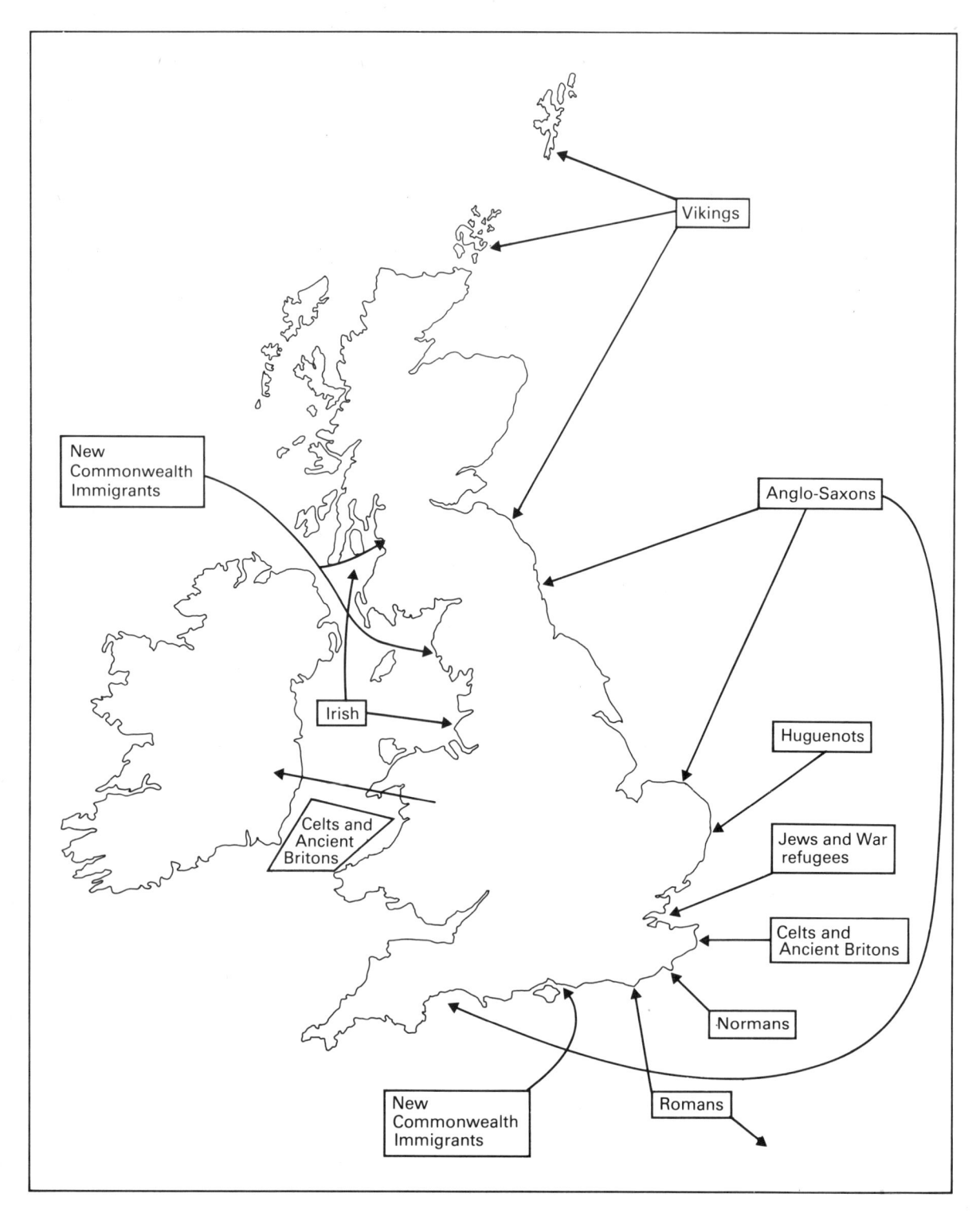

The British are a mixture of races

24 INTRODUCING SOCIAL STUDIES

New Lanark in Robert Owen's time

could make the best of themselves if only they had a perfect world in which to live. In the fourth century BC, a Greek thinker called Plato wrote about an ideal city in his *Republic*. It was a place where everybody would work willingly together for the good of all. The family would be abolished and men and women would not live together in separate households. Children would be brought up communally, and women released from domestic chores to work in the wider community. All people would do the work to which their abilities made them best suited.

The setting up of any ideal society depends upon *cooperation* with people jointly struggling to find the best solution to our problems.

In the last century, Robert Owen had marvellous ideas about building villages of cooperation where individuals worked together for the good of the community. He began a cooperative colony called New Harmony in the USA, but it ended in failure because of the imperfections of its inhabitants. His villages of cooperation in Britain were called parallelograms; the community was supposed to live harmoniously within the shape made by their houses, while they grew their food on the lands outside.

In New Lanark, in Scotland, Robert Owen established a factory of cooperation where all the people would have the opportunity to give of their very best. He rewarded the women by giving baskets of goods to those who kept their houses clean. He was one of the first to start infant schools for children who worked in his cotton spinning factory. Owen was a great believer in developing character. Those who worked well and honestly, proudly displayed white cards over their machines, but those who were idle, or who swore, had black cards. There were shades of colour for those in between. In its heyday New Lanark had 2000 inhabitants; today only about eighty people live in this Scottish ghost town.

You may have read William Golding's *Lord of the Flies*. A group of boys are marooned on a desert island. What a wonderful chance to create an ideal society.

> Ralph turned to the others.
> 'This belongs to us....'
> 'While we're waiting we can have a good time on this island.'
> He gesticulated widely.
> 'It's like in a book.'
> At once there was a clamour.
> 'Treasure Island....'
> Ralph waved the conch.
> 'This is our island. It's a good island. Until the grown-ups come to fetch us we'll have fun.'
> WILLIAM GOLDING, *Lord of the Flies*

Their 'fun' turned into murder as each individual boy changed when left without help and guidance. What do you think is meant by the statement below?

> 'Each man has a wild beast within him.'
> FREDERICK THE GREAT

As a person you have to live in a world full of imperfect people of whom you are one. You must try to recognise the possibilities for good and bad in yourself and in others. A person's failure to make the best of himself leads to all kinds of personal and emotional problems. Schools employ welfare officers and counsellors to help you sort them out. Teachers feel responsibility and concern for you during adolescence. For adolescence is a time for exploring and discovering; a time to find the real you; a time to make the best of yourself.

This poem on adolescence was written by a fourteen-year-old girl at the Hewett Comprehensive School, Norwich:

Adolescence

> Adolescence is a time for being the greatest, for doing things you've never done before, for thinking things you've never thought before.
> Adolescence is a time for exploring, for exploring yourself and your surroundings.
> Adolescence is a time of discovery, of new inventions, of great ideals.
> Adolescence is a time of awareness, of opening your eyes, tasting, touching, smelling, hearing, learning.
> Adolescence is the opening of a flower lain so long underground and in a tightly closed bud.
> Adolescence is a new, broader world with new horizons. All that was once hidden is now in view. Oh, who but fools would hinder the wakening of a sleeping child?
>
> CHRISTINE POMFRET

There are four choices you can make:

1 You can REJECT society – opt out, drop out, give up, go and live in a monastery or a convent where the world's problems will pass you by.
2 You can DREAM about a pleasant impossible world in some such place as the Big Rock Candy Mountains.

> O... the... buzzin' of the bees
> In the cigarette trees,
> Round the sodawater fountains,
> Near the lemonade springs,
> Where the whangdoodle sings
> In the Big Rock Candy Mountains.

3 You can ACCEPT the challenges of living in an imperfect world full of imperfect people of whom you are but one.
4 You can join existing groups or organise yourselves into new ones to help CHANGE the society in which we live towards a more ideal society.

Here is a translation of a fourteenth-century prayer:

> Give us serenity to accept what cannot be changed;
> Courage to change what should be changed,
> And wisdom to know one from the other.

Things to do and think about

1 Draw a map of your perfect island. Either use the conventional signs used by geographers or make up some of your own. Provide a simple key.
2 Read this poem by John Lennon and then try writing one of your own beginning, 'Imagine...'

> imagine no possessions
> i wonder if you can
> no need for greed or hunger
> a brotherhood of man
> imagine all the people
> sharing all the world
>
> you may say i'm a dreamer
> but i'm not the only one
> i hope some day you'll join us
> and the world will be as one

3 Paint a picture called 'A better world'. Here are some ideas:
test tube babies
escalator roads
moon holidays
space cities
pills for food
world government
personal helicopters
free goods
Atlantic Tunnel
1000-storey skyscrapers
clothes that never wear out
more electronic gadgets
no disease
no war
no strikes
no racial discrimination
no sex discrimination
no class distinction
no slavery
no money
no cripples
no mental illness
no pollution
no death
Be prepared to reject some of the ideas and to add some of your own.

4 Cut out 'get away from it all' advertisements from colour magazines and make an attractive collage. Do you think the claims made in the advertisements are honest?

5 Read Luke, chapter 15, verses 11–32 and tell, in your own words, the story of the prodigal son. What do you think is meant by the phrase, 'Then he came to his senses' (*New English Bible*) or 'when he came to himself' (*Authorised Version*)?

6 Collect topical press cuttings to illustrate:
(a) anti-social acts (i.e. unhelpful)
(b) pro-social acts (i.e. helpful).
You may find the newspapers give more space to anti-social acts. Why is this? Try to 'balance' your cuttings – say six of each.

7 Name three types of handicap which prevent some people making the best of themselves. Suggest ways in which their handicaps might be overcome.

8 Imagine that you are an Irishman, a Welshman or a Scot, and point out what you consider to be the special contributions of your people to the British nation. Do you think these are grounds for separate parliaments?

9 Give reasons for your belief about the right and wrong of the following situations:
(a) It is all right to kill in wartime.
(b) People who are dying, and in great pain, should be put out of their misery.
(c) Both girls and boys should be beaten if they behave badly.
(d) Where possible old people ought to be looked after by their own families and not put into homes.
(e) Hanging IRA bombers would only result in more revenge murders.

Terms used in Unit 1

unique	environment
differences	causality
conform	instincts
group norms	homo sapiens
conflict	evolution
hypothesis	natural selection
roles	experiences
role conflict	values
modification	biological drives
heredity	cooperation

Further examples of terms used in the social sciences are given at the end of each unit. You will find it useful to enter them in a book and write the meaning in your own words against each one.

UNIT 2
You and your family

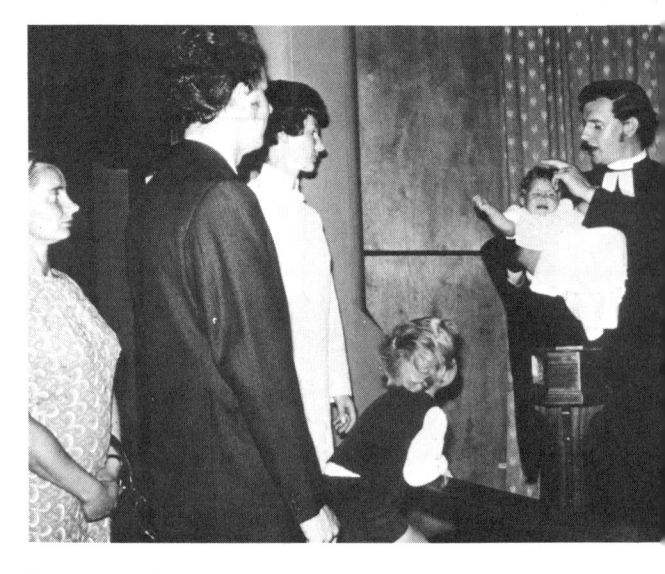

Baptism makes a person a member of the Christian Church — what rites makes people members of other faiths?

TOPIC 2.1 **Your relations**

In the photograph who is the person most interested in the baptism? It seems to be the baby's brother. He is getting quite excited about the whole thing. Perhaps he's thinking, 'I've not seen baby washed with all her clothes on before'. Or do you think he's glad she's crying? After all he didn't cry when he was baptised. Probably he thinks it is all a game.

Father and mother look very serious. It is an important occasion for them. They are agreeing that their child will be brought up according to the teaching of the Christian religion. Many parents want their children to understand beliefs and customs that support the *traditions* of their society.

This baby's family will expect her to behave in certain ways, which they will teach her. The process by which she learns what is expected of her is called *socialisation*. She will also come to expect certain behaviour of her family.

If you had been born in a different country, you would be expected to obey different rules and customs. What religion(s) would you

28 INTRODUCING SOCIAL STUDIES

Christianity
Jesus Christ AD1–33
the Bible

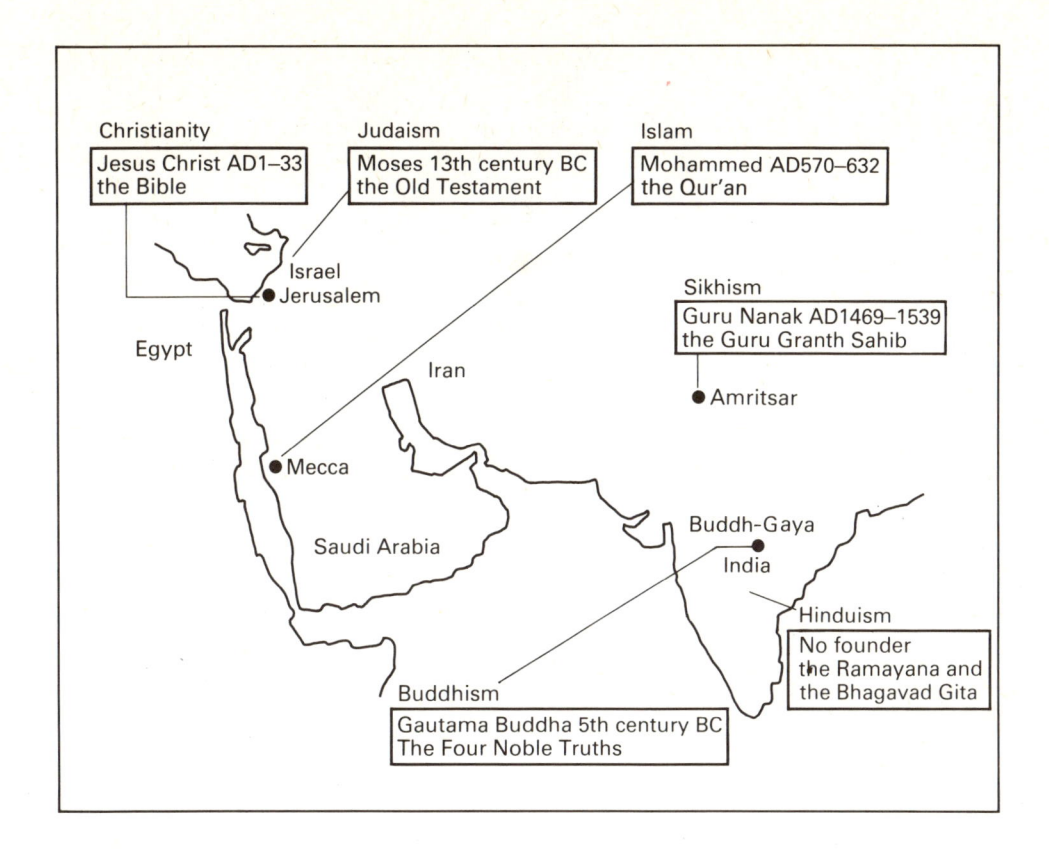

Judaism
Moses 13th century BC
the Old Testament

Islam
Mohammed AD570–632
the Qur'an

Sikhism
Guru Nanak AD1469–1539
the Guru Granth Sahib

Hinduism
No founder
the Ramayana and
the Bhagavad Gita

Buddhism
Gautama Buddha 5th century BC
The Four Noble Truths

The main religions of the world and their countries of origin

most likely have been taught to believe in if you had been born in:
(a) India   (d) Israel
(b) Egypt   (e) Greece?
(c) Japan

In whichever country people are born, they are most likely to be members of a family and have relations.

> Most people in any society are born into a family. Each has a mother and a father, who themselves have mothers and fathers. Mothers and fathers have brothers and sisters. Children have children. Brothers and sisters have children. So each individual has a set of people, different from every other individual who is related to him (or her) by 'blood'.
> RONALD FRANKENBURG, *Communities in Britain*

The young child is influenced by the people with whom she lives. She takes them as examples of how to behave. For most people, socialisation takes place mainly within the family circle. The baby in the picture will copy her brother who has already learnt a lot from their father and mother. Both children will look to their parents for the final *authority* – for the final say in the matter. Until they reach the age of eighteen, when they become adults, the children will be under the care of their parents, in the eyes of the law.

We are also influenced by friends of the family. Who is the other woman in the photograph of the baptism? Is there anything which makes you think she is a relative? What are the duties of a godmother?

YOUR RELATIONS 29

'We're playing mothers and fathers.'

A typical modern family – why is it smaller than the Victorian one?

A typical Victorian family

Mother, father and 2 children

Nuclear family live apart from relatives

Husband and wife are equal partners

Children have more freedom

The life style of a typical modern family

Years ago families were much larger than they are today. How many people can you count in this family portrait of 1865?

The average family in Victorian days had about seven children. How many brothers and sisters have you? How many friends can you think of with more than four brothers and sisters? Nowadays it is customary for families to be quite small. Why?

In modern Britain a family usually consists of a husband and wife and their children. The photograph above right shows such a group; sociologists refer to it as a *nuclear family*.

30 INTRODUCING SOCIAL STUDIES

The *extended family* includes grandparents, uncles and aunts, cousins and other relations, and sometimes they all live under one roof. In Borneo it is usual for extended families to live together in a longhouse which might contain about 500 people. In Britain today there are still examples of extended families living together but it is not as common as it used to be. The way in which some London families used to live together is described by Michael Young and Peter Willmott in a book called *Family and Kinship in East London* (Penguin, 1957).

> Because they have lived in it for so long, most Bethnal Greeners are surrounded by scores of people they know very well, people who are one minute relations and another minute neighbours, another minute friends, another minute counsellors. The emphasis is not so much on the individual home, prized as this is, as on the informal collective life outside it in the extended family, the street, the pub and the open air market.
>
> In a place like Bethnal Green you can find several generations of families and their relatives. They may live, work and spend their leisure together....
>
> In Bethnal Green many families continue to act together as a single unit. The young people look after their parents when they are old. Newlyweds often live with the wife's parents; the daughter goes out to work or to shop, leaving the children with mother. When advice is needed, 'Mum' is at hand. The tie between mother and daughter is very strong: here the old proverb is very true: 'My son's a son until he gets him a wife, my daughter's a daughter all her life.'

The more relatives who live together, the more people there will be to share in the upbringing of the children. It is a matter of cooperation or working together. Dr Margaret Mead in *Coming of Age in Samoa* suggests that many children are a lot happier in Samoa than they would be growing up in a Westernised nuclear family where conflicts may be caused because parents and children live so close together that they get on one another's nerves. Children in Samoa are brought up with several men and women to care for them and so they naturally turn to older brothers and sisters, to uncles and aunts and especially to grandparents. Also the roles of children are more clearly defined in Samoa, particularly through the difficult transition periods, e.g. during adolescence, and there is less conflict at that age in Samoa than in the Western nuclear family.

> The close relationship between parent and child, which has such decisive influence upon so many in our civilisation that submission to the parent or defiance of the parent may become the dominating pattern of a lifetime, is not found in Samoa. Children reared in households where there are half a dozen adult women to care for them and dry their tears, and a half dozen adult males, all of whom represent constituted authority, do not distinguish their parents as sharply as our children do.
>
> MARGARET MEAD, *Coming of Age in Samoa*

Can we 'learn from a picture in which the home does not dominate and distort the life of the child'? Are there any times when you would be happier if you lived in a larger family and had more relations sharing your life? What would be some of the disadvantages?

The children you see on page 32 who are cleaning their own classroom live in an Israeli kibbutz at Shomrat. In a kibbutz many families live together and the grown-ups share in raising the children. It is another example of cooperation.

In Britain, family relationships are usually clear-cut and definite. Most of you regard your mother and father, brothers and sisters as your closest relations. You probably do not see your uncles and aunts or cousins very often. If your grandparents are still alive how often do you see them?

A baby is born completely helpless and needs to have everything done for it. A very close relationship builds up between the baby

Cleaning the classroom is a kibbutz child's contribution to doing community chores

and the person who cares for it. That person is usually the mother, but the role is sometimes taken over by a mother-substitute, who may be an adoptive or foster mother, or the father.

Child care or mothercraft is a subject taught at many schools, but the relationship of love cannot be taught. In your earliest days, which you no longer remember, your mother expressed her love by the way she fed you, touched you, cared for you. As your feeling of well-being and confidence developed you learned to love her because she loved you.

Nowadays the father takes more part in parenthood than he did at the beginning of this century. He may be present at the birth of his son or daughter; he often helps with the care of the baby, e.g. changing nappies and bathing; he takes an interest in his child's development and education; he spends time playing with his child; and because a mother can get very tired attending to young children all the time, the father sometimes looks after them completely or takes them for outings to let the mother relax. In some families the father stays at home with the children while the mother goes out to work.

Sometimes there is only one parent or perhaps the father's job takes him away from home for long periods of time. In these circumstances the one parent takes over the role of both father and mother.

When people depend on each other for the satisfaction of their needs we call this *interdependence*. A parent gains satisfaction from loving, and the children gain satisfaction from being loved. As children grow up and pass through different stages in the *life-cycle* the form of loving undergoes *changes* or modifications. They become more independent of their parents, but still need their support and guidance, particularly through stages like adolescence.

There are special relationships between the children of a family. Each one has a certain *status* or order of rank, which usually depends on age. The eldest child sometimes assists the parents by helping to care for the younger ones, and they in turn learn from their older brothers and sisters.

There are bound to be conflicts or areas of difficulties between brothers and sisters. The older ones may think that the youngest is spoiled. Younger ones may feel that the 'special privileges' of the older children, such as being allowed to go to bed later and having more pocket money, are unfair.

One child in a family may be better at some things such as music and singing, while another may be good at games. In this way, children learn within the family unit that there are many struggles in life, struggles between their own desires and the needs of others.

It is within this small family group that a child first experiences *social control*, which means the controlling of his behaviour and the resolving of struggles so that he can live amicably with the rest of his family. Parents

32 INTRODUCING SOCIAL STUDIES

'I shall marry a man like my dad – he's easy to bully.'

help to deal with the jealousies and rivalries of their sons and daughters, and encourage them to live as unselfishly as possible. By this sort of socialisation you learn to live in a more or less unselfish way with other people. If you can learn to deal with conflicts between yourself and other members of your family, it will be easier to deal with the many other conflicts which are bound to arise in later life.

Things to do and think about

1. Carry out a survey of the different patterns of family life among the members of your class, e.g. how many have:
   (a) one-child families, two-child families, etc.
   (b) brothers and/or sisters in each family
   (c) one-parent families?

2. Read the passage below:

   > In Kino's head there was a song now, clear and soft, and if he had been able to speak of it, he would have called it the Song of the Family.
   >
   > His blanket was over his nose to protect him from the dank air. His eyes flicked to a rustle beside him. It was Juana arising, almost soundlessly. On her hard bare feet she went to the hanging box where Coyotito slept, and she leaned over and said a little reassuring word. Coyotito looked up for a moment and closed his eyes and slept again.
   >
   > ... The Song of the Family came now from behind Kino. And the rhythm of the family song was the grinding-stone where Juana worked the corn for the morning cakes.
   >
   > The dawn came quickly now, a wash, a glow, a lightness, and then an explosion of fire as the sun arose out of the Gulf.
   >
   > Kino heard the creak of the rope when Juana took Coyotito out of his hanging box and cleaned him and hammocked him in her shawl in a loop that placed him close to her breast. Kino could see these things without looking at them. Juana sang softly an ancient song that had only three notes and yet endless variety of interval. And this was part of the family song too. It was all part. Sometimes it rose to an aching chord that caught the throat, saying this is safety, this is warmth, this is the Whole.
   >
   > JOHN STEINBECK, *The Pearl*

   What does the author mean when he says about the family, 'this is the Whole'?

3. How is family life affected by:
   (a) neighbours
   (b) religious beliefs
   (c) squabbles?

4. Do some research in your school library or public library and then give an account of family life in:
   (a) Victorian days
   (b) Borneo
   (c) Samoa or New Guinea
   (d) London or some other large city or town.

5. What do you think would be the advantage and disadvantages of living in a kibbutz, for:
   (a) a mother   (c) a son
   (b) a father   (d) a daughter?

6   In your opinion:
    (a) What family jobs should be done by children?
    (b) Should pocket money be according to age, chores done – or what?
7   In what ways is the arrival of another child into a family likely to affect:
    (a) the mother
    (b) the father
    (c) the other children?
8   How are family relationships likely to be affected if mother goes out to work?

9   Prepare a talk to be given on *one* of the following subjects:
    (a) The father must be the head of the family.
    (b) It is silly to say, 'Children should be seen, but not heard'.
    (c) All members of the family can be equal, although they have different roles to fulfil.
    (d) Most modern families are too 'child-centred'.

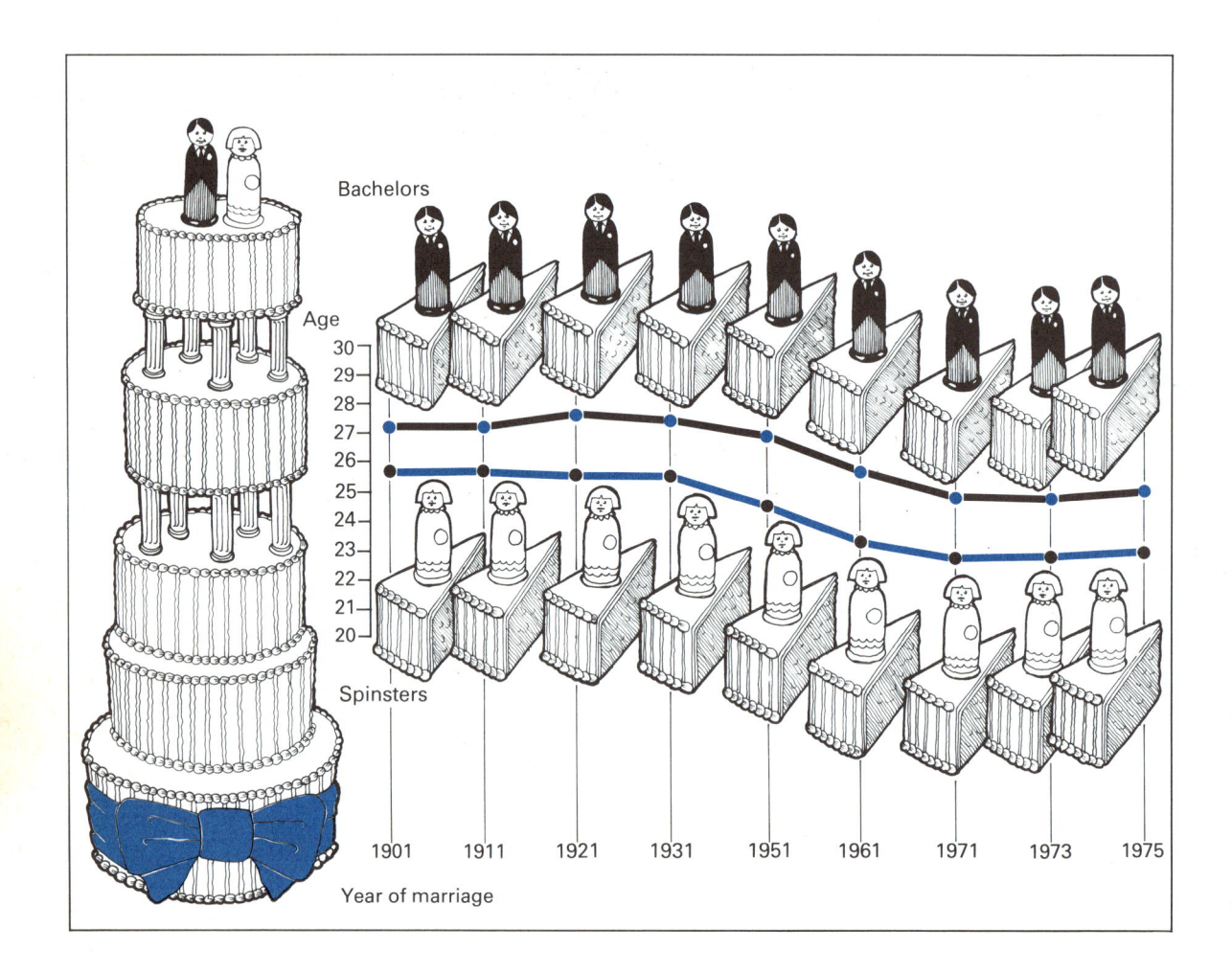

Women marry earlier than men

34   INTRODUCING SOCIAL STUDIES

TOPIC 2.2 Families

Look at the picture of the wedding party in the African state of Cameroon. The wedding party blocks the highway and all the traffic has to stop. Each person is supposed to present a gift to the bride. It is a happy occasion.

Why do people get married? What makes a happy marriage? In many parts of the world marriages are still arranged by the families of the couple for many different reasons. Even in recent British history, marriages were arranged among the landed and wealthy to merge large fortunes and estates. Wealthy merchants would try to find husbands for their daughters among the gentry, hoping to raise their social and economic status. Are parents likely to make a wiser choice of marriage partners for their children than young people are likely to do for themselves? Can you think of reasons against this idea?

All over the world people are often expected to marry within their own occupational and social group. How true is this of our own country today?

Look at the bride's family in the picture. Look at the groom's. What is different about the two families?

In Russia after the revolution of 1917, an attempt was made to abolish the family. The experiment failed because the ordinary people were against it. So the state had to accept the family as an important and permanent part of national life.

> The family is, and always has been, the most intimate and one of the most important of human groups ... it can be said to be universal.
> RONALD FLETCHER, *The Family and Marriage in Britain*

The family is the most common human group in many countries of the world. How can family life make people happy? Does it fulfil people's basic human needs? We know that not all families are happy, because many

Which is the middle-class and which the working-class family at this wedding?

FAMILIES 35

marriages end in divorce. The divorce rate doubled between 1960 and 1970, and doubled again between 1970 and 1977 when 9 in every 1000 marriages ended in divorce.

People sometimes do not wish to live in family units, but choose to live in other groups of people. Can you think of any alternatives to the nuclear family?

The family as we know it in Britain tends to consist of a mother, father and two or three children. There are always variations on this. Sometimes one parent is absent, through death or separation. There may be fewer or more children, or perhaps no children at all.

A happy family is a good environment in which to rear children. Many couples who get married want to have children. Many see it as a *natural function*. As we saw in Topic 2.1, when we are children we learn from our own parents and brothers and sisters how to resolve the conflicts which arise in the family. The interests of several people living so closely together often clash, and by struggling to overcome our difficulties amicably, and by learning from our parents how to get on with each other, we become socialised.

When children arrive in a marriage, they

'I can't wait to be grown-up and able to do exactly as I please.'

'Hello Mr Brown! Mrs Brown had her baby yet?'

bring a lot of changes. Usually the wife had been working up to that time, so there is the loss of one income, at least for a while. The baby is very demanding on the parents' time and emotions. The parents find they are restricted and cannot go about freely as they used to. But the joys of producing their children generally make these changes seem unimportant.

The young child needs care and affection and most parents freely give it. It is essential

> that the infant and young child should experience a warm, intimate and continuous relationship with his mother (or mother-substitute) in which both find satisfaction and enjoyment. The child needs to feel he is an object of pleasure and pride to his mother.
> JOHN BOWLBY, *Child Care and Growth*

The pleasure of giving to their children often brings couples close together.

Not all families have children. One couple in six find they are unable to produce children. They may adopt or foster a child. Or couples may decide that they both wish to continue working and have no family at all. Do you think the family unit can truly exist for a couple without children?

As babies grow they show curiosity and a desire to learn things. Parents and children together can enjoy each stage in the process of growing up. The first few years of a child's life are very important for laying the basis on which it develops its future skills and personality. A family can provide love, education, recreation and relaxation for all its members.

The modern family is smaller than families

of the past. Until this century many babies and children died in infancy, and couples had large families in the hope that some of the children would survive. This idea is strong today in some developing countries. Modern medicinal care and hygiene enable most babies in the Western world to live and grow up to become adults. But modern couples are also able to use contraception to limit the number of children they produce. This is called family planning. There are many family planning clinics all over the country, and they offer free advice on contraception to anyone who wants it.

Nobody knows you better than the members of your family. They have summered and wintered you. They get impatient with you sometimes, but they also allow for your weaknesses and are probably the first to come to your support if you are criticised or attacked by people outside the family. Most families possess a keen sense of loyalty towards their members.

Members of a family can find working together enjoyable. Jobs about the home are shared. From an early age children will be expected to perform family chores. This is a form of the *division of labour* and we shall see how it is a very important part of life. For example, in a factory different workers do different jobs and the final product is the result of cooperative effort.

One of the functions of the family has always been to provide a place for relaxation. The Victorian family had musical evenings where each member of the family was expected to sing or perform on a musical instrument. Some modern families share similar talents and join together in providing entertainment, or in playing games together, taking outings in the car, watching television or going away for holidays.

Some functions of the family

FAMILIES 37

Let us sum up the things which the family does:
1. provides a good environment for child-rearing
2. socialises children in their early years
3. trains and educates the young for life in society
4. offers opportunities for support, enjoyment and relaxation.

Things to do and think about

1. 'Home, sweet home.' With this motto in mind, list ways in which your home has helped to prepare you for adult life.
2. Make a collage to illustrate the theme 'family life' by collecting and arranging pictures from newspapers and magazines.
3. In what ways is a child's life in the traditional family likely to differ from that in:
   (a) an orphanage
   (b) an Israeli kibbutz
   (c) a commune?
4. At what age do you think people should get married? Give your reasons.
5. Compare your home life with that of:
   (a) a medieval serf
   (b) a modern royal princess.
6. Discuss among your friends the subject of 'family life'. Include questions on:
   (a) time spent at home
   (b) jobs done
   (c) rewards and punishments
   (d) family holidays.
7. What are the advantages and disadvantages of bringing up a family while living:
   (a) with in-laws
   (b) in a high-rise flat
   (c) in accommodation shared with friends
   (d) a gypsy life?
8. Give reasons for and against young people (under the age of eighteen) being required to secure parental consent for marriage.

TOPIC 2.3 Family conflicts

On a tired housewife

> Here lies a poor woman who was always tired,
> She lived in a house where help wasn't hired;
> Her last words on earth were: 'Dear friends, I am going
> To where there's no cooking, no washing, or sewing,
> For everything there is exact to my wishes,
> For where they don't eat there's no washing of dishes.
> I'll be where loud anthems will always be ringing,
> But having no voice I'll be quit of the singing.
> Don't mourn for me now, don't mourn for me never,
> I am going to do nothing for ever and ever.'
>
> ANON.

Conflicts are bound to arise when several individuals live under one roof. From time to time there will be squabbles between members of the family and with neighbours and other relatives.

> The people upstairs all practise ballet.
> Their living room is a bowling alley.
> Their bedroom is full of conducted tours.
> Their radio is louder than yours.
> They celebrate weekends all the week.
> When they take a shower, your ceilings leak.
>
> OGDEN NASH

When conflicts arise in the family, it is unlikely that there will be a single cause. Let us imagine that a child lines up ten soldiers one behind the other and then they all fall down. What causes number ten to fall down? It was knocked down by number nine, but it was knocked down by number eight which was knocked down by number seven and so on until we trace the cause back to the first soldier to fall. Why did it fall? Perhaps another child pushed the soldier over on purpose, or slammed the door hoping the soldiers would all collapse. Was this because yesterday the child playing with the soldiers had done something to annoy the other one?

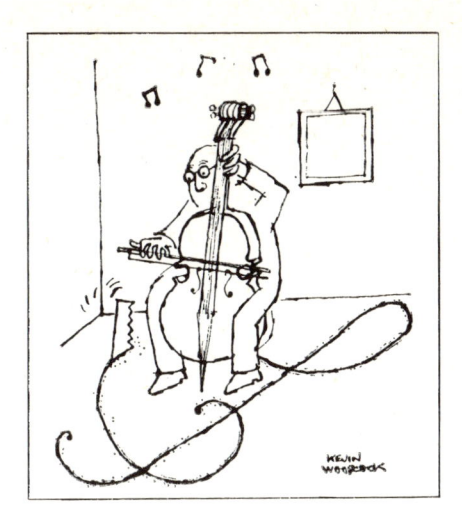

We have seen that people have different experiences and different motives or reasons for actions. The first child may feel that he is not wanted any more when another child appears in the family. The elder one now has to share his parents' love with a brother or sister. It is natural that mother has to give the new baby a great deal of time and attention because it is so helpless. The parents can help the older child to adjust to the new baby by letting him help with looking after it. They can show the older child that he is just as important to them as he ever was, and encourage him to delight in the new arrival.

These are two ways in which we can see that conflict is not simply caused by one event. There are so many *environmental factors* which affect us, the way we feel and the way we behave. The relation between cause and effect is very complex. The newspapers give a lot of space to things like wife-beating and baby-battering. Why do people do these things?

'BABY FOR SALE'
Father killed her when the deal fell through, court told

A YOUNG father tried to sell his baby daughter for £100 then battered her to death after the deal fell through, a court heard yesterday.

Mr X, aged 23, an unemployed miner, wanted to sell his five-month-old baby, Toni, to save him from sleepless nights caused by her crying, Leeds Crown Court was told.

Agony of kids 'treated like footballs'

UNHAPPY couples are treating children like footballs, a report claimed yesterday.

Some youngsters are often battered and kicked unmercifully, said Mrs Jean Moore in a survey for the National Society for the Prevention of Cruelty to Children.

Trapped

She added: 'It is almost as if the parents take out their misery on the children who become the footballs of the marriage.'

Mrs Moore, who investigated 32 cases, said that child victims fell into three categories:

THE ELDEST child who parents felt had trapped them into a painful marriage.

THE CHILD who has the same 'failings' as one of its parents and is punished for them.

THE DISTURBED child, like the little boy beaten for playing with matches because his mother was anxious he should not cause a house blaze for the second time.

The children at greatest risk are aged between five and eight, said Mrs Moore. They are not only beaten by hand, but with weapons.

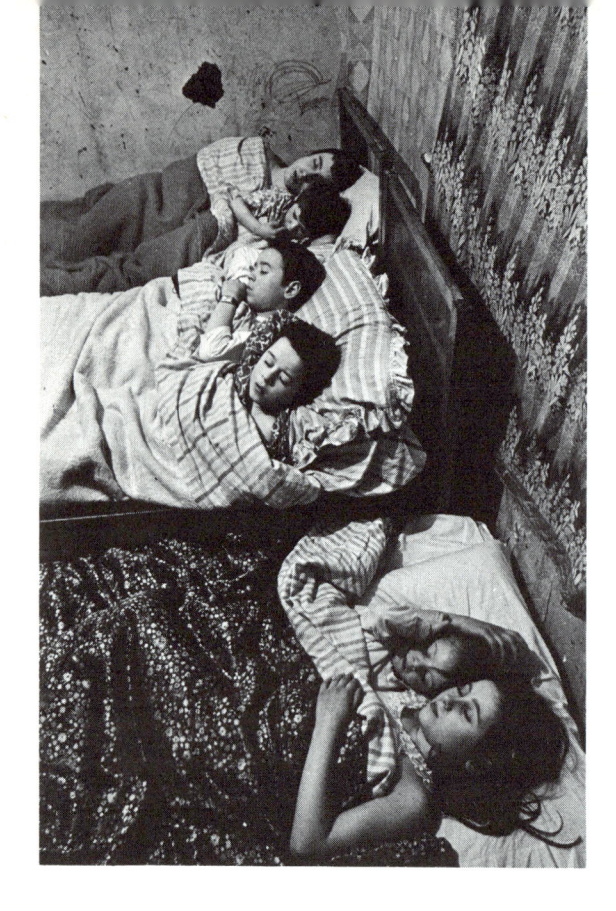

This room is officially overcrowded yet people still have to live in these conditions

It would be easy to think that they do these things because they are wicked. But that is far too simple. Did the man beat his wife because she provoked him to do it, or because he is an over-aggressive man? Did she provoke him? Maybe she had had a hard day with the children, living in cramped conditions, with not enough money. Is the husband over-aggressive? Maybe he came home from work exhausted and wanted to relax and have his meal in peace and quiet but the children were too noisy. Where does the cause lie? Is it bad temper – or bad housing? Who is responsible for the bad housing?

But again the housing may not be bad. It may be unsuitable. We talked in Topic 2.1 about the families in Bethnal Green. Young and Willmott also studied the same families when they were moved out of their 'slum' dwellings into modern high-rise flats in new towns, in the country with plenty of space and fresh air. That sounds ideal. But was it? The people missed the social life of Bethnal Green and all that went with it – chatting over the garden wall, support from the extended family for mothers with young children, the local pub, and the corner shop. The people had lost their roots when they moved into their new and better housing. Some people were unhappy. There was a lot of vandalism and delinquency.

These are the sorts of questions that we as social scientists ask to try to find out the cause and effect of behaviour in societies.

Perhaps the reason why some people beat their wives and babies has nothing to do with the immediate environment. The parents may have ideal home conditions, plenty of space, and enough money but had unhappy child-hoods, and found themselves unable to cope with the emotional strains and conflicts within their own families when they grew up.

So you see conflict can have many causes, many more than we have talked about and not always the ones we might expect.

In the picture a husband separated from his wife struggles on his own to bring up five children.

Conflict between parents leads to misery. The little boy in the photograph is a victim of a broken home. He was left in a London hotel bedroom on Christmas Day. Fortunately there were people to care for him at the Otterden Reception Home in Camden. Our photograph shows him protected by wire netting and holding a toy gun in each hand. He is a victim of conflict.

Can you think why his parents might have rejected him? When a family is unable to resolve the conflict within it, sometimes it is better for all the members of the family to break up, rather than live under intolerable strain.

What problems could a father have bringing up a family alone?

Even in the protection of a Home an abandoned child can find Christmas lonely and confusing

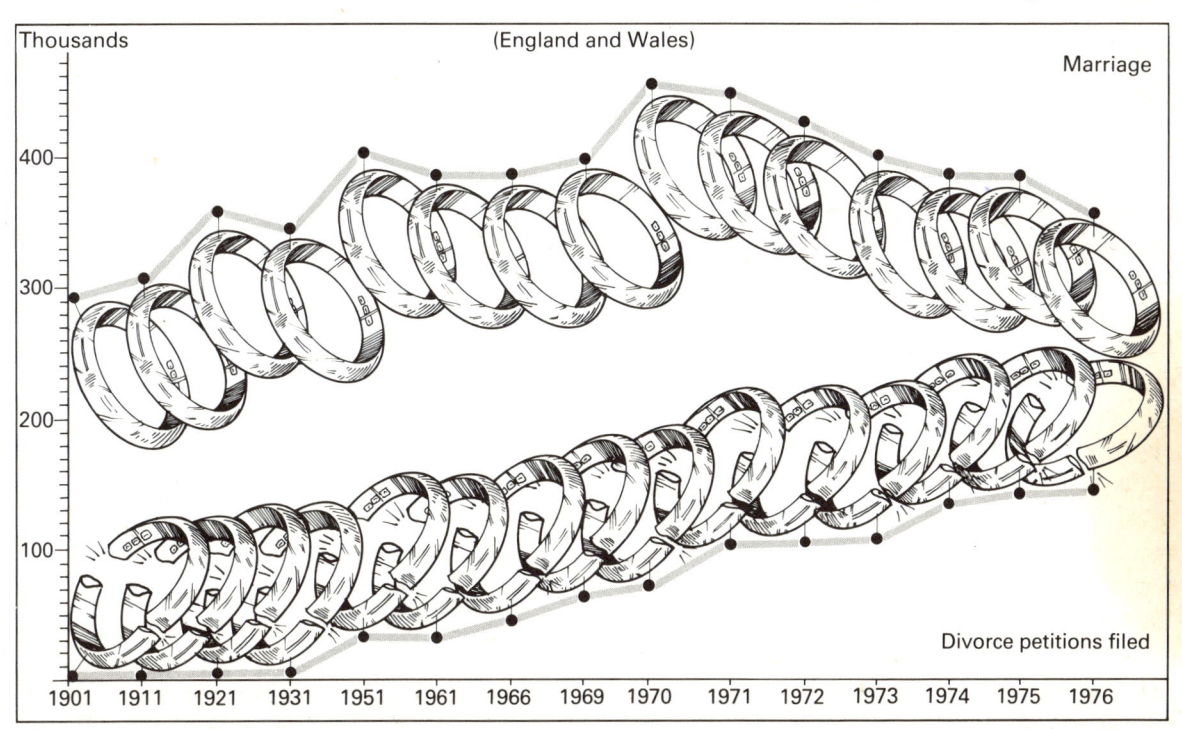

Thousands (England and Wales)

Marriage

Divorce petitions filed

1901 1911 1921 1931 1951 1961 1966 1969 1970 1971 1972 1973 1974 1975 1976

Marriage is increasing but so is divorce

FAMILY CONFLICTS 41

Things to do and think about

1. List some radio or TV programmes which are based on family conflicts.
   (a) Which of these programmes do you listen to or watch?
   (b) Why do you watch them?
   (c) Are they realistic?
   (d) How could they be improved?
2. Prepare a talk on one of the following topics:
   (a) Divorce is wrong in all circumstances.
   (b) Divorce should be allowed in some circumstances.
   (c) A woman's place is in the home.
   (d) A father and mother should share equally in bringing up the children.
3. What does a marriage guidance counsellor do?
4. Do you think that divorce should be easier for childless couples than for parents of young children? Give reasons for your answer.
5. Which do you think is better? To be brought up:
   (a) by guardians
   (b) in a children's home
   (c) by foster parents
   (d) by a lone parent?
6. In cases of cruelty, what can be done to help children and parents?
7. Read chapter 4 of Charles Dickens's *David Copperfield*, and then write your opinion of Mr Murdstone.
8. Write an imaginary conversation between two parents. The father wants his parents to live with them but the mother is against it.

Terms used in Unit 2

traditions
socialisation
authority
nuclear family
extended family
interdependence
life-cycle

changes
status
social control
natural function
division of labour
environmental factors

42 INTRODUCING SOCIAL STUDIES

UNIT 3
You and your friends

TOPIC 3.1 Being a teenager

Do you always act your age? In the last unit we looked at the *social development* of the individual as a member of a family. We have seen how you are influenced by heredity and environment and that by cooperation you are encouraged to develop the sort of behaviour that grown-ups think is fitting for your age. Do your parents ever tell you to 'grow up'?

Parents and their children often disagree about how quickly young people should grow up. Some parents think their children are developing too quickly and try to hold them back. You may have been told off for adopting the latest fashion. Both girls and boys may be told to be in earlier at night. Parents usually have the best interests of their children at heart but they have to realise that as people grow up they need more independence. They want to live their own lives and choose their own friends.

Consider your best friend and your worst enemy. What are they really like? Jot down words which help to describe them, *as people*. For instance, cheerful or miserable, cruel or kind, brave or cowardly, a 'sticker' or gives up easily. The words you have chosen describe someone's *personality*.

'Yes, our generation has a lot to answer for – YOUR generation.'

BEING A TEENAGER 43

Teenagers face lots of problems. This is true for girls and boys, but let us consider a teenage girl. She has her own special thoughts, fears, hopes and feelings and she looks for someone with whom to share them. At the age of about thirteen she is likely to turn to members of her own age group (i.e. her *peer group*), because she feels they are likely to understand her best. After all, they have similar problems. Teenagers like to get together in *groups*.

Don't make the mistake of thinking that your teenage problems are peculiar to you. Your friends will often be in conflict with their parents or teachers. At home and school young people are expected to pay attention to those in authority over them. It is difficult for those to whom you have turned for advice for many years to realise that you want to get along on your own.

Little Johnny's final letter

Mother,
   I won't be home this evening, so
Don't worry; don't hurry to report me missing.
Don't drain the canals to find me,
I've decided to stay alive, don't
search the woods, I'm not hiding,
simply gone to get myself classified.
Don't leave my shreddies out,
I've done with security.
Don't circulate my photograph to society
I have disguised myself as a man
and am giving priority to obscurity.
It suits me fine:
I have taken off my short trousers
and put on long ones, and
now am going out into the city, so
don't worry; don't hurry to report me missing.

I've rented a room without any curtains
and sit behind the windows growing cold,
heard your plea on the radio this morning,
you sounded sad and strangely old. . . .

BRIAN PATTEN

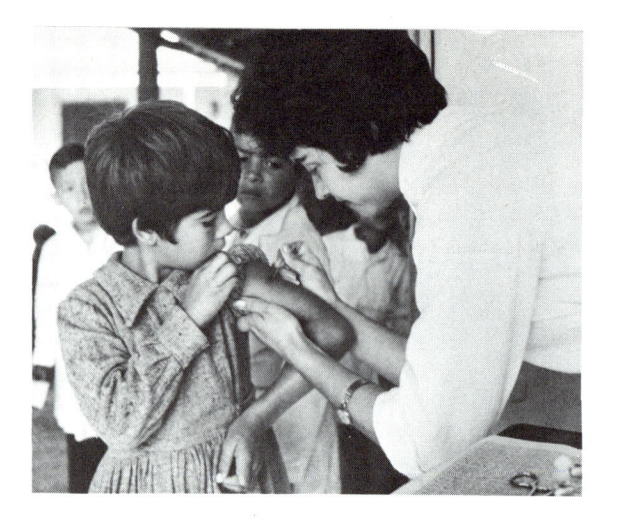

A school immunisation session – what is the relationship between the child and the adult here?

How does the relationship between the adult and children here differ from that in the photo above?

There was a time when an adult was needed to stop you from scalding yourself with boiling water, or doing a hundred other different things which would have been against your own interest. At the teenage stage

44 INTRODUCING SOCIAL STUDIES

a *generation gap* may develop. You probably prefer being with a group of people of your own age, young people also, though sometimes adults may be able to help you.

Young people's relationships with adults change.

You will know that while you are a teenager changes take place in your body and your mind. Being neither a child nor an adult you can feel awkward in the company of both. Adults may consider you 'difficult' yet many of the difficulties are caused by the environment in which we live.

Margaret Mead, the anthropologist, studied teenagers in the simple society of Samoa. One thing she noticed was that the change from childhood to adulthood was less complicated there. The boys carried on hunting and fishing as they had done since they were quite young. The girls continued cooking and weaving and baby-minding. These adult responsibilities had been theirs since a very young age.

Contrast these people, living in a non-industrial society, with those in a modern society such as ours where young teenagers are not regarded as ready for *adult roles*. These attitudes are reflected in social controls, in the form of laws, preventing young people from doing various things, as you can see on page 46. You cannot leave school or get married until you are sixteen. You are not allowed to vote or consume alcoholic drink in a public house until you are eighteen. What arguments can you put forward against the fact that a person is allowed to get married and become a parent at sixteen but is not thought fit to vote until the age of eighteen? What changes, if any, would you make to these laws?

It is very natural to turn to your teenage friends because they share the same language, the same ideas and the same hopes. When children become teenagers they seek from their friends the security they once sought mainly from their families. Perhaps you can add to the following table of differences between families and friends.

Differences between family and friends

Your family 'picked' you by accident of birth.	You choose your friends.
Families consist of both old and young people.	Your friends are in your own age groups.
Parents are 'heads' of the family.	Your friends may have a natural leader or no leader at all.
The family supplies shelter and food.	Your friends supply companionship.
People remain part of a family throughout life.	Your friendship patterns change. New friends are made, old friendships forgotten.

Things to do and think about

1 When you are an adult what important decisions will you make which will change your life?

2 How far are your ideas about:
 (a) drinking (b) drugs (c) gambling (d) sex and (e) smoking, similar to or different from the ideas of your parents? If they differ, why do you think this is so?

3 Design a poster to illustrate how you can help *either*:
 (a) those younger than yourself
 or (b) the elderly.

4 Is there much of a generation gap between you and the very old and the very young? Why do you think a generation gap frequently exists between teenagers and their parents?

5 Suggest reasons why young people often feel 'awkward' at the age of thirteen or fourteen.

Age 21 Stand for election to Parliament

Age 13 Undertake part-time employment

Age 19 Join the police force

Age 14 Be on licensed premises but not drink alcohol

Age 18 Vote and buy alcohol

Age 15 Open a National Giro account

Age 17 Learn to drive a car

Age 16 Marry with parental consent

What you can do legally

46 INTRODUCING SOCIAL STUDIES

TOPIC 3.2 Friendships

(*The scene is a parent–teacher interview.*)

Mr Chalk (*the teacher*). Ah now, you're Colin's dad, I believe.

Mr Dadd (*the parent*). Yes, that's right, and I'm not very happy about how Colin is getting on since he came to this comprehensive school.

Mr Chalk. I'm sorry to hear that. Is he finding the lessons difficult?

Mr Dadd. No, he's getting on all right with his school work but he's mixing with the wrong sort.

Mr Chalk. We've got all sorts here. What's wrong with Colin's friends?

Mr Dadd. To start with they use language.

Mr Chalk. We all use language, Mr Dadd; that's the way we communicate.

Mr Dadd. You know what I mean. Colin is beginning to use bad language. Words he didn't learn at home. He never hears his mum or me speak like that.

Mr Chalk. I'm sorry to hear this, but Colin mixes with all sorts of children. No doubt he picks his own friends.

Mr Dadd. Well, I would like you to stop him seeing Fred Bloggins. I happen to know that his elder brother is on probation. They are a right bad lot, those Bloggins. Fred's father is a drunkard. They are not the same class as my boy. We've brought him up proper and we don't want him getting into bad ways.

Mr Chalk. If Colin has been taught the right things, Mr Dadd, perhaps he will help Fred to mend his ways. Fred hasn't had much of a chance. It will be good for him to mix with a boy like Colin.

Do you quarrel with your parents about your choice of friends? Do you think Mr Chalk was right that if Colin had been brought up so well he should be able to resist any bad *influences*?

By the time young people reach adolescence, the influences of other groups are sometimes stronger than those of the home. Young people find that the school, their friends and even television meet the needs of their changing outlook and ideas, and in comparison their parents sometimes seem out of date.

This gap is part of the growing away from parents that is inevitable as you grow up and become more independent. Each of us has to learn to pick the *lifestyle* that suits us best.

However, the generation gap of the teenage years is not usually a challenge to the fundamental ideas and values with which we have been brought up. We saw how the early years are important in forming a person's personality, and it is usually the values we have learned in our childhood which continue to influence us throughout our lives. So we are usually not so very different from our parents.

A fine example of *friendship* is found in the story of how 'Titus' Oates gave his life in an attempt to save the friends who accompanied him on his journey to the Antarctic. Captain Scott and his party made their way successfully to the South Pole, but on the return journey they were overcome by freezing blizzards and terrible frostbite. Entries from Scott's diary show what kind of a friend Titus Oates was.

10 March 1912 Things steadily downhill. Oates' foot worse. He has rare pluck and must know that he can never get through. He asked Wilson if he had a chance this morning, and of course Bill had to say he didn't know. In point of fact he has none....

11 March 1912 'Titus' Oates is very near the end, one feels. What we or he will do, God only knows. We discussed the matter over breakfast; he is a fine, brave fellow and understands the situation, but he practically asked for advice. Nothing could be said but to urge him to march as long as he could.

16 March 1912 This was the end. He slept through the night before last, hoping not to wake; but he woke in the morning – yesterday. It was blowing a blizzard. He said, 'I am going outside and may be some time.' He went out into the blizzard and we have not seen him since....

We knew that he was walking to his death, but though we tried to dissuade him, we knew it was the act of a brave man and an English gentleman. We all hope to meet the end with a similar spirit, and assuredly the end is not far.

'Titus' Oates's heroic act of friendship was not enough to save Scott and his other two friends, Wilson and Bowers. But Oates could have done no more.

A police constable once had the task of catching a murderer who had escaped from Broadmoor Mental Prison. When the man on the run was cornered, he fired his gun and the police constable was blinded. After having been awarded the George Cross for arresting this dangerous man who might well have murdered again, the constable was asked if he would have done the same thing if he had known that he would have been made blind. He replied that he would have acted in the same way even if he had known beforehand. He acted in the interests of all of us, i.e. of the whole *community*. (See Unit 5.) Collect some stories from newspapers about people who have risked their own safety for others.

It is sometimes said of a good man that he is a friend of all mankind but usually friendship is a very personal thing. Friendship satisfies a deep-felt need for human *companionship*. Have you ever thought what life would be like on a desert island? There would be no one to touch, no one to talk to, no one to laugh and sing with, no one to play with.

Have you ever visited an old, lonely person who gripped your hand and wouldn't let go? Perhaps you felt most embarrassed. As a teenager you probably have lots of friends and it is hard to appreciate what it is like to be lonely and feel a need for the friendship of other human beings. Young people can help a lot. Look at the picture of the young man feeding the old one. Who do you think is getting the most satisfaction?

It is possible to be lonely and friendless in a crowd. Try reading Albert Camus' *The Outsider* (Penguin). It is about a man who is surrounded by people but whom nobody really knows.

Would you like to go on holiday on your

'Who will come and play football?'

In what other ways can you give and get satisfaction from a relationship with an older person?

48 INTRODUCING SOCIAL STUDIES

Three youngsters enjoying a holiday together

Things to do and think about

1. (a) What ideas have you exchanged recently with friends?
   (b) What dreams of the future have you shared with friends?
2. A broken friendship can hurt a lot. What would you do if:
   (a) you felt that you had outgrown a friend
   (b) you wanted to try to patch up a broken friendship?
3. Often friends are very much alike. Choose one of your friends and suggest ways in which you are alike. Why is it possible for 'opposites' sometimes to be friends?
4. Make a list of the qualities you value in a friend, e.g. cheerfulness, truthfulness, looks, etc. Put them in order of importance. Now compare your list with your neighbours'.
   Give reasons to the rest of the class why you have placed a certain quality:
   (a) at the top of the list
   (b) at the bottom of the list.
5. Collect advertisements which make use of the word 'friendly'. For example, the 'friendly drink' or the 'friendly shop'. Do you think the word 'friendly' has been used in the true sense?
6. Compare the following ideas which are important when choosing a friend and write 1, 2, 3, etc. against each according to how you rate them:
   (a) the same age
   (b) the same sex
   (c) the same form, class or tutor-group
   (d) being related
   (e) personality.
   Why did you rate number 1 as your first choice?
   List things that friends can do for you, e.g. stand by you; share things with you.

own? You could join the crowds sunbathing on the beach, but you would find it difficult to be happy without any friends. The youngsters in the photograph look happy. Whatever they are going to do, they expect to do it together.

When people depend upon each other for satisfaction, social scientists call this *interdependence*. Make a list of the most important people you depend on for happiness. How many of them are friends of your own age group?

You need your friends to help you grow up. Without friends you may become very shy and reserved. Look up the word 'introvert' in a dictionary. Are you an introvert? Have you friends in whom you can confide and with whom you can dream?

FRIENDSHIPS 49

7 Study the photograph of the four children and make up a story about them.
8 Draw or paint a picture illustrating the proverb: 'A friend in need is a friend indeed'.
9 Friends often form themselves into groups. See if you can find out about the following groups:
Hell's Angels
hippies
Friends of the Earth
rockers
skinheads.

Terms used in Unit 3

social development	influences
personality	lifestyle
peer group	friendship
groups	community
generation gap	companionship
adult roles	interdependence

UNIT 4
You and your education

TOPIC 4.1 What should be taught?

We have seen that by socialisation we learn how the people around us want us to behave. A child learns to say 'please' and 'thank you'; she finds that she is more likely to get what she wants if she follows these customary ways of *social behaviour*. From the beginning of our lives we learn to live with other people and act according to what is thought to be good and bad or right and wrong in our society. What we learn depends upon the type of society into which we are born. We learn what sociologists call the *culture* of the society – the ideas, values, habits and traditions which are passed on from generation to generation.

Education varies as cultures vary. There are many differences between what children learn in a *non-industrial society* compared with what they learn in an *industrial society*. Examples of these differences may be seen by making comparisons between life in a society such as that of the Hadza people of Tanzania with life in modern Britain. The Hadza are a very simple people whose lives depend on their surroundings or environment. They also socialise their children in what they consider to be right or wrong. In the same way as in an industrial society, they pass on the ideas, values, habits and traditions to future generations. But the education needed for survival differs between the two types of society. The Hadza are nomads wandering from place to place. They live by gathering fruits and berries or by hunting African wildlife. They depend on cooperation. They have to be self-sufficient so there is very little trading with other tribes. The possessions of the Hadza are simple: bows and arrows, axes, hunting knives, digging sticks, cooking utensils.

Try to make your own comparison between what people would be expected to learn in such a society and what you have had to learn in our society. In a society in which there is no

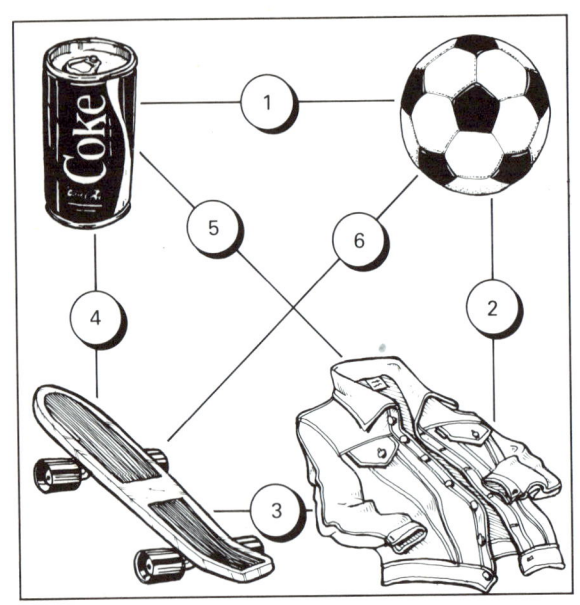

To swap 4 things you need 6 exchange rates. How many exchange rates would you need to swap 5 things?

trade or industry there would be no need to learn about money and shops and cars and factories. The Hadza do not have to learn to read or write; they have no books so they pass on knowledge by word of mouth. They use basic *methods of communication*. The parents and other elders teach the children their *traditional skills*. There are no schools. The Hadza rely upon the patterns of behaviour and customs which have lasted for centuries.

It takes a long time for changes to take place in a society. Cultures never remain still and are always having to be changed or adapted to meet fresh circumstances. We call this *cultural change*. For example, the Hadza are now making shoes from old rubber tyres. This is a new skill which had to be learnt; it is no longer so important to learn to capture eland or zebra from which they used to make footwear. They now swap their honey for metals with which they make knives and axeheads. This swapping is known as *exchange*.

New skills are being taught and old ones are forgotten. As the Hadza come into closer contact with other societies, cultural changes will increase and no doubt one day they will have to conform to the industrialised way of life in other parts of Tanzania. This will mean they must learn such *basic education* as reading and writing. The government hopes to set up schools in Hadza areas. When the children grow up and become parents they will be able to teach their own children what they have learned in schools.

When you learn anything from mother and father, brothers and sisters, relations and friends, it is called *informal education*. A type of informal education has been well described by E. J. and J. D. Krige in a passage about the education of the children of the Bantu tribe.

> Children learn the tasks required of adults simply by doing them. They are anxious to imitate their elders, and there is never any compulsory element in the teaching of these skills. Moreover in their education they have this advantage, that it is not carried on in an institution divorced from everyday adult activities. The child feels that he is an essential part of society....
>
> E. J. & J. D. KRIGE, *The Realm of a Rain Queen*

In time the Hadza people may spend less time with their children because they will not need them to help with the hunting and gathering. As cultural change speeds up, the Hadza may find themselves working on farms and in factories. Then the children would

You can learn things by simply doing them – what is the woman doing here?

52 INTRODUCING SOCIAL STUDIES

become separated from their parents during the day and have to rely mainly upon *formal education* or organised schooling. One day perhaps they will have classes and lessons just as you do.

We can now see how the change to industrialisation can affect people's lives. Do you think the changes are for the better? Do you think the children would be happier learning about money and arithmetic than they were helping with hunting and fishing? Their education will probably be simply to read, write and do arithmetic. What sort of jobs will this lead to? Would they be interesting?

On these two pages are photographs of children receiving informal education. Write down the things you think these children are learning. All the time we are growing up we are learning from everything we do.

A Jewish child learning mealtime prayers

An Indian girl helping her mother in the family shop

Do you work to raise extra money for yourself or others?

Playing can be learning

Do you attend school just to acquire *knowledge*? Do you think that the main thing you should learn at school is a lot of facts? Or are you more concerned with how to USE the facts – and the skills – which you acquire? Have you ever thought of the differences between knowledge and *intelligence*?

If you watch TV quizzes or a programme such as *Mastermind*, perhaps you are sometimes amazed at the knowledge of the competitors. The contest is won by the person who knows the most facts. But intelligence is the ability to think things out for yourself. By doing this you *use* the facts which you know; but just acquiring knowledge means you simply *store* the facts. Contrast the TV programme *Mastermind* with the game of the same name. The Mastermind game requires intelligence because you have to think and work out what your opponent has done.

Let us consider the differences between knowledge and intelligence a little further. Some years ago there was a series of broadcasts by a performer who called himself 'The Memory Man'. If he was asked the winner of the Grand National in 1921, he was able to rap out the answer. He was also certain to know the winner of the Boat Race and the FA Cup in that year, or in any other year you cared to mention.

Do you think it is valuable to accumulate an enormous number of facts? Or do you think it is better to know where to find the information you require? Which of these alternatives does your school place most emphasis on?

> The main lesson in school is how to get along in the world. Different subjects are merely means to this end. In the olden days it used to be thought that all a school had to do was make children learn to read, write, figure, and memorise a certain number of facts about the world. . . . You learn only when things mean something to you. One job of a school is to make subjects so interesting and real that the children want to learn and remember.

You can go only so far with books and talk. You learn better from actually living the things you are studying. Children pick up more arithmetic in a week from running a school store, giving change, and keeping the books, than they learn in a month out of a book of cold figures.

There's no use knowing a lot if you can't be happy, can't get along with people, can't hold the kind of job you want. The good teacher tries to understand each child so that she can help him overcome his weak points and develop into a well-rounded person. The child who lacks self-confidence needs chances to succeed. The trouble making show-off has to learn how to gain the recognition he craves through doing good work. The child who doesn't know how to make friends needs help in becoming sociable and appealing. The child who seems to be lazy has to have his enthusiasm discovered.

A school can go only so far with a cut-and-dried programme in which everyone in the class reads from page 17 to page 23 in the reader at the same time and then does the examples on page 128 of the arithmetic book. It works well enough for the average child who is adjusted, anyway. But it's too dull for the bright pupils, too speedy for the slow ones. It gives the boy who hates books a chance to stick paper clips in the pigtails of the girl in front. It does nothing to help the girl who is lonely or the boy who needs to learn cooperation.

DR BENJAMIN SPOCK, *Baby and Child Care*

So an individual needs to learn the best ways of living his life to the full and how to cooperate with other individuals in society so they also get the utmost out of life. Education should be concerned with each person having, as far as is possible, an equal chance – this means *equality of opportunity*. You want to learn how to keep your body fit, your brain active and your emotions under control. This is a threefold way of looking at education – one needs to learn how to develop as fully as possible: (a) physically; (b) mentally; (c) spiritually.

Although equality of opportunity is an educational ideal, we do not possess equal talents, and it would be a dull world if we did.

The differences, which supply the essential mix of human variety, would not exist.

But there are also other reasons why the opportunity for equality is not available. We saw in Unit 2 how important our home life is for our development. Some children are at a disadvantage because they come from poor homes and get little encouragement from their families. They may not be able to use the opportunities provided by the school to their best advantage. Also, the schools themselves vary in the quality of education offered.

Things to do and think about

1. We have seen in this topic that what is learned by the Hadza has altered with cultural changes. Research in the library then list ways in which the British way of life has changed since 1870, and how the education of British people has changed as a result.
2. Give some examples of how you were informally educated before starting school:
   (a) by parents
   (b) by other relatives
   (c) by friends of your own age.
3. What is the Dewey classification system? See if you can find out how it works.
4. Use your school or public library to find what Dewey classification number you would look under if you wanted to learn more about the different branches of social science:
   (a) anthropology (study of man)
   (b) economics (study of the distribution of scarce resources)
   (c) ethics (study of the moral principles which govern social behaviour)
   (d) psychology (study of the origins, development and forms of behaviour)
   (e) sociology (study of man's behaviour as part of a social system).

Look up each word in a dictionary and write down the definitions.

5. Try to match these statements and pictures:
   (a) An educated person has learned to entertain *him-* or *herself*. b) An educated person has learned to entertain *others*. (c) An educated person has learned to entertain *an idea*.

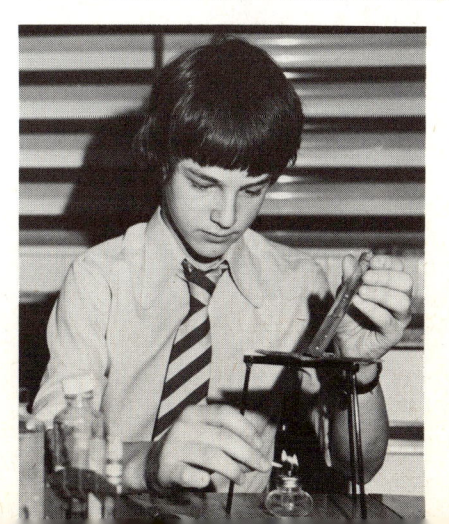

6 Keep an account of the most important things you have learned during one complete day, making a note of times, places and activities.

7 Make a similar record to the one you worked out for yourself in number 6 above, on one of the following:
(a) a two-year-old
(b) a five-year-old
(c) a seven-year-old.

8 From the following statements select those:
(a) with which you agree
(b) with which you disagree
(c) about which you are unsure.
Give reasons for your choices.
 (i) Children at school play too much nowadays.
 (ii) Pupils ought to decide the subjects which should be taught.
 (iii) A teacher should not tell other teachers anything which a pupil relates in confidence.
 (iv) A school must have some standards of right and wrong.
 (v) Pupils should be treated equally.
 (vi) Pupils should not be forced to do physical activities.
 (vii) Corporal punishment is always bad.
 (viii) Nobody should be forced to go to school.

9 Draw a strip cartoon to illustrate these educational stages as suggested by the psychologist Jean Piaget:

Up to 2 years
Motor actions – child discovers things by touching and feeling

2 to 7 years
Language – child understands signs and symbols

8 to 11 years
Tangible things – child comprehends areas and volumes

12 years onwards
Abstract concepts – child aware of ideas such as freedom and justice.

10 Suggest ways in which you would cope with:
(a) teaching a small child to count
(b) making peace between two quarrelling toddlers
(c) looking after a pedestrian injured in a street accident.
Which of the things you have already learned would you be able to use? What new things might you learn from these activities?

11 As a group, discuss these views of what a child should know:

> A child must know the rules of the road, be able to read placards and publications, fill voting papers, compose and send letters and telegrams, purchase food and clothing and railway tickets for itself, count money and give and take change, and generally know how many beans make five. It must know some law, were it only a simple set of commandments, some political economy, agriculture enough to shut the gates of fields with cattle in them and not to trample on growing crops, sanitation enough not to defile its haunts, and religion enough to have some idea of why it is allowed its rights and why it must respect the rights of others. And the rest of its education must consist of anything else it can pick up, for beyond this society cannot go with any certainty.
> BERNARD SHAW, *Misalliance*

TOPIC 4.2 Going to school

Most children in Britain go to school for the first time at the age of five. There will always be a conflict about whether or not this is the best age to start formal schooling. In 1972, Mrs Margaret Thatcher (then Secretary of State for Education and Science) introduced a ten-year programme in a document called *Education: A Framework for Expansion*. The

A pre-school playgroup, an opportunity for young children to begin socialising

intention was to offer nursery education to all 2–5 year-olds whose parents thought it a good thing. It is unlikely that you attended a nursery school but in the future there may be more nursery schools available for your younger brothers or sisters. They may already be going to pre-school play groups.

Do you think that a young child is likely to receive a better education at home or will she be better provided for at school? Your answer will probably depend upon the ideas you have about home environment. At school she will learn the need for cooperation with children of her own age and with the adults who teach her. She will also begin to learn the traditions and values of society at large. Will these necessarily be the same as those she learns at home? She will learn a great deal about interdependence, about how we rely upon each other. School discipline acts as a social control and will help to shape and modify an individual's behaviour, character and personality. In the Greek state of ancient Sparta, children of seven were taken from their parents and brought up with others of the same age by an officer selected by the government for the task.

Do you remember your first day at school? Did you like it? Did you feel like the little boy described in *Little Children* by William Saroyan?

'I like you,' the housekeeper said.
'Then why are you taking me to school?' he said.
He had taken walks with Amy before, once all the way to the Court House Park for the Sunday afternoon band concert, but this walk to school was different.
'What for?' he said.
'Everybody must go to school,' the housekeeper said.
'Did you go to school?' he said.
'No,' said Amy.
'Then why do I have to go?' he said.
'You will like it,' said the housekeeper.
He walked on with her in silence, holding her hand. 'I don't like you,' he said. 'I don't like you any more.'
'I like you,' said Amy.
'Then why are you taking me to school?' he said again.
'Why?'
The housekeeper knew how frightened a little boy could be about going to school.
'You will like it,' she said. 'I think you will sing songs and play games.'
'I don't want to,' he said.
'I will come and get you every afternoon,' she said.
'I don't like you,' he told her again.
She felt very unhappy about the little boy going to school, but she knew that he would have to go.

Schools have changed enormously over the years. They were once such dreadful places that it is not surprising that children dreaded not only their first day at school, but every other day as well. Consider Charles Dickens's description of Dotheboys Hall which appears in his novel *Nicholas Nickleby*:

'There,' said the schoolmaster as they stepped in together, 'this is our shop, Nickleby!'
It was such a crowded scene, and there were so many objects to attract attention, that, at first, Nicholas stared about him, really without seeing anything at all. By degrees, however, the place resolved itself into a bare and dirty room, with a couple of windows, whereof a tenth part might be of glass, the remainder being stopped up with old copybooks and paper. There were a couple of long old rickety desks, cut and notched, and

inked, and damaged, in every possible way; two or three forms; a detached desk for Squeers; and another for this assistant....

But the pupils – the young noblemen! How the last faint traces of hope, the remotest glimmering of any good to be derived from his efforts in this den, faded from the mind of Nicholas as he looked in dismay around! Pale and haggard faces, lank and bony figures, children with the countenances of old men, deformities with irons upon their limbs, boys of stunted growth, and others whose long meagre legs would hardly bear their stooping bodies, all crowded on the view together; there were the bleared eye, the hare-lip, the crooked foot, and every ugliness or distortion that told of unnatural aversion conceived by parents for their offspring, or of young lives which, from the earliest dawn of infancy, had been one horrible endurance of cruelty and neglect....

... Mr Squeers looked very profound, as if he had a perfect apprehension of what was inside all the books, and could say every word of their contents by heart if he only chose to take the trouble, that gentleman called up the first class.

Obedient to this summons there ranged themselves in front of the schoolmaster's desk, half-a-dozen scarecrows, out at knees and elbows, one of whom placed a torn and filthy book beneath his learned eye.

'This is the first class in English spelling and philosophy, Nickleby,' said Squeers, beckoning Nicholas to stand beside him. 'We'll get up a Latin one, and hand that over to you. Now, then, where's the first boy?'

'Please, sir, he's cleaning the back parlour window,' said the temporary head of the philosophical class.

'So he is, to be sure,' rejoined Squeers. 'We go upon the practical mode of teaching, Nickleby; the regular education system. C-l-e-a-n, clean, verb active, to make bright, to scour. W-i-n, win, d-e-r, der, winder, a casement. When the boy knows this out of the book, he goes and does it. It's just the same principle as the use of the globes. Where's the second boy?'

'Please, sir, he's weeding the garden,' replied a small voice.

'To be sure,' said Squeers, by no means disconcerted. 'So he is. B-o-t, bot, t-i-n, tin, bottin, n-e-y, bottinney, noun substantive, a knowledge of plants. When he has learned that

Dotheboys Hall

bottinney means a knowledge of plants, he goes and knows 'em. That's our system, Nickleby; what do you think of it?'

'It's a very useful one, at any rate,' answered Nicholas.

'I believe you,' rejoined Squeers, not remarking the emphasis of his usher.

'Third boy, what's a horse?'

'A beast, sir,' replied the boy.

'So it is,' said Squeers. 'Ain't it, Nickleby? Nickleby?'

'I believe there is no doubt of that, sir,' answered Nicholas.

'Of course there isn't,' said Squeers. 'A horse is a quadruped, and quadruped's Latin for beast, as everybody that's gone through the grammar, knows, or else where's the use of having grammars at all?'

'Where, indeed!' said Nicholas abstractedly.

'As you're perfect in that,' resumed Squeers, turning to the boy, 'go and look after my horse, and rub him down well, or I'll rub you down. The rest of the class go and draw water up, till somebody tells you to leave off, for it's washing-day tomorrow, and they want the coppers filled.'

So saying, he dismissed the first class to their experiments in practical philosophy, and eyed Nicholas with a look, half cunning and half doubtful, as if he were not altogether certain what he might think of him by this time.

'That's the way we do it, Nickleby,' he said, after a pause....

Dotheboys Hall was a typical school for less privileged children of the mid-nineteenth century. Charles Dickens was writing from experience because he had taught in a similar school himself. The *evidence* of people who have actually taken part in anything is very vital to the social scientist. In the late nineteenth century most schools were called Board Schools because they were run by School Boards whereas today schools are organised by local education authorities (LEAs). 'The Board School,' wrote one writer, 'was not much of a place.'

> I went to the Board School when I was exactly four years old. The place smelt of disinfectant and disapproval. I learned nothing except how to fight and swear. I could curse horribly long before I knew that C.A.T. spells CAT.
>
> CASSANDRA *John Bull's Schooldays*

Children at a modern nursery school find out, through direct experience, some of the things which they will learn more about later from teachers and books. Much of the time is given to free *experimental activity*; through play, children begin to acquire the skills necessary for further learning. Individual and co-operative investigations help them to understand their environment. Remember that the first five years are of tremendous importance. During this time the seeds of future educational advances will be sown.

Look at the photograph of the infant school in Nottingham. When children build with odd bits of material, they compare shapes and sizes and weights and distances. If left to themselves they will begin to discuss the problems that arise in their constructions. They learn to help each other. They learn cooperation and interdependence.

Now that you have reached the secondary stage in education, you have gone a long way towards mastering the three Rs (reading, writing and arithmetic) and you should be in a position to begin to question and put a value on what you are taught and the purpose of it all. Would you agree that the three Rs are still worthwhile? Are employers and universities right when they complain about declining standards of English? How would you go about improving children's ability to handle numbers? Or is self-confidence more important than being able to handle language and numbers?

There are so many things that have to be crammed into a school curriculum that it is very important to make the best possible choice between what is included and what is left out. *Scarcity* of time and resources affect our whole lives. If you decide what you think should be taught at your school, then it will be easier to judge whether or not you think your school is doing a sound job. Remember it is only your opinion. Your parents, teachers and friends would probably express differences of opinion.

The following objectives for secondary

What do you think these children are learning?

Changes they'd like to see in the schools

MARGARET ALLISON, our Sixth Form Forum contributor, takes a look at the views and aims of the National Union of School Students and finds that their basic objective is to improve schools for the benefit of the pupils. This, she says, is how they believe it could be done.

The National Union of School Students has received some bad publicity in the past, so I talked to Lee Gladwell, chairman of one Norfolk grammar school branch, to get the student view.

The basic aim of the N.U.S.S. is to improve schools for the benefit of the pupils. They hope to move towards a completely comprehensive school system – based on continuous assessment rather than exams. They feel that it is a much fairer system when students are not segregated according to their examination performance.

CHOOSING

Because there wouldn't be any exams., they hope that pupils would be allowed to study only the parts of the course in which they were really interested, thus ensuring the continuing interest of the majority of pupils. They also believe that there should be more student participation in deciding the subjects of lessons, as well as in the general running of the school.

They want the feudal system of authority in schools to be abolished in favour of a committee made up of staff, students, parents, and possibly professional people, such as psychologists; and that all these people should be elected.

LEARNING

I was told that the N.U.S.S. think that students should not attend school for the sole purpose of learning facts but actually to learn how to learn for themselves. 'We want schools to be places which will stimulate interest and a desire to learn,' they say.

The N.U.S.S. do not approve of the prefectorial system, believing that self-discipline should be encouraged. They also think that sixth-formers shouldn't have any special privileges which are denied to the rest of the school.

The N.U.S.S. was set up to give students a chance to do something about things in their schools with which they were unhappy. School councils had prepared the ground, but the head master still had the right to veto any motion passed by the council.

Firstly, they must show that a majority are dissatisfied with something; then proposals for change are made to the head master and staff. If nothing comes of this, they have to gain more support and publicity through leaflets, petitions and mass meetings.

DECIDING

Lee told me that any school can form a branch of the N.U.S.S. if they have four people interested. All the schools send representatives to area conferences, and there is a national headquarters in London.

The feelings of the N.U.S.S. members are perhaps summed-up in the following slogan: 'Students should decide their fate, not the head and not the State.'

Strong views – but the silent majority remain unimpressed.

---

schools were drawn up as part of a survey for the Schools Council. Copy them down and then number them in order of importance.

To help you do as well as possible in examinations like GCE or CSE.

To teach you things which will be of direct use to you in your job.

To teach you things which will help you to get as good a job or career as possible.

To teach you about different sorts of jobs and careers so that you can decide what you want to do.

To help you to know what it will be like when you start work, for example, about hours and conditions.

To take you on visits to factories or offices or other work places to see the different sort of jobs there are and what the work is like.

To teach you things that will be useful in running a home, for example, about bringing up children, home repairs, decorating.

To teach you how to manage your money when you are earning, and about things like rates and income tax.

To give sex education.

To help you to learn how to get on with other people, for example, those you work with, your future wife or husband.

To teach you to speak well and easily.

To teach you to be able to put things in writing easily.

To help you to become independent and able to stand on your own feet.

To help you develop your personality and character.

To teach you about what is right and wrong.

To teach you how to behave so that you will be confident and at ease when you leave school.

To help you to make the most of yourself, for example, with your appearance.

To help you to know about what is going on in the world nowadays.

To teach you plenty of subjects so that you can be interested in a lot of things.

To give you interests and hobbies that you can do in your spare time.

To take you on visits to places like the local fire station or town hall to learn what is going on in the world outside school.

To run clubs that you can go to out of school hours.

To take pupils away on holidays.

To arrange courses in which pupils live away from home for a while.

To take you on outings to places like art galleries, the theatre, museums or castles.

To do drama in school, that is, acting or reading plays.

To study poetry in school and read or learn poems.

'Where?', the magazine of the Advisory Centre for Education

Your school is not just concerned with imparting knowledge. It is also interested in your character, personality, conduct and welfare. A good school wants its students to have inquiring minds.

Things to do and think about

1. Winston Churchill suggested that nobody should begin formal schooling before the age of 14! Suggest some advantages and disadvantages of starting school at 14.

2. Prepare a plan for building an ideal school. The suggestions below are given to help you. Use them if you wish, but you will probably have other ideas of your own. Areas for:
   audio-visual aids
   social studies
   indoor sports
   arts and crafts
   libraries
   seminars (small learning groups)
   computer science
   refreshments
   music and drama
   team-teaching

3. 'I should like to go to a school where you are free to use your own initiative and learn things for yourself.'
   (a) What could you say for and against this statement?
   (b) Use your library to find out about A. S. Neill's Summerhill School. (See *That Dreadful School* by A. S. Neill.) Would you like to attend a school like Summerhill?

4. In what ways is your school organised so that pupils are taught according to their:
   (a) age
   (b) ability
   (c) interests?

5. The 1975 Bullock Report *A Language for Life* came to the conclusion that standards of reading fall below present-day needs. What suggestions can you make for improving the teaching of the English language?

6. How much importance does your school attach to teaching you about:
   (a) the laws of our society
   (b) the customs and festivals of our society
   (c) making your way in the world?

A tic-tac man working on a race course

7 Prepare a talk which would provide a stimulating opening for a discussion on *one* of the following topics:
(a) Co-education (mixed schooling) is the most natural way of organising education.
(b) Adolescent boys and girls learn more in separate (i.e. single-sex) schools where there are fewer distractions.

8 What do these methods of class organisation mean:
(a) banding
(b) setting
(c) streaming?
Which have you experienced? Which do you prefer? Why?

TOPIC 4.3 Communicating

Throughout your life you have been learning through acts of communications. Education is a matter of communicating knowledge, ideas, beliefs, customs.

You do not have to use words in order to communicate. The man in the photograph is communicating some complicated knowledge by *non-verbal communication*. What sort of facts is he passing on by his signals?

Touch is an important method of non-verbal communication. A baby spends so much time close to its mother or mother-substitute, that it begins to realise that mother loves and cares for it. Bodily contact such as cuddling or smacking affects the way a child learns about the behaviour expected of it.

As you grow up you become involved in more complicated non-verbal communications. Have you ever been called to the Head's study? If so there has probably not been much body-proximity or close contact. He may have remained seated behind a desk while you stood and faced him. His relationship with you may not have been over friendly but there may well have been respect between the two of you. When a boy puts his arm round his girl he wants to communicate

62 INTRODUCING SOCIAL STUDIES

What different methods of communication can you find here?

warm feelings towards her through touch. In this way he 'tells' her something, and she learns by his communications.

The eyes play a vital part in *social interactions*. When you look somebody 'in the eye' it may help you to learn about his or her emotional state. The eyes can be used to communicate fear, horror, surprise or amusement. What do you understand by: 'He gave her a knowing look' or 'She looked very understanding'? The length of time spent in looking is another indication of the intimacy of human relationships. What are face-to-face communications? Apart from the eyes the whole of the human face may change as we communicate and receive different messages by facial expressions. The direction of looking is also important when communicating; MPs must 'catch the Speaker's eye' before he calls them to speak in the House of Commons. The tone of your voice is another vehicle of communication. A depressed person is likely to communicate his emotional state by a slow and monotonous expression, while a highly excited person speaks quickly in a high-pitched voice. Hand and foot movements are also used to communicate something. Have you ever watched the hands and feet of someone who is nervous? If you want to stop communicating you can remove your whole body from the scene by just walking away.

Communications play a vital part in your education throughout the whole of life. A baby learns some things by non-verbal communications, but it is able to learn far more when it understands the meaning of words. We saw in Unit 1 how language has allowed humans to develop far beyond the furthest stage reached by any other species.

At school you learn by a variety of means of communication. Your teacher talks to you, or writes words on a blackboard, or presents them to you on a wallchart, or arranges for you to listen to a radio or to watch a television programme or see a film. In turn, you respond

COMMUNICATING 63

in a variety of ways. You may appear interested or bored. You may show you have understood the teacher. You may ask questions and by these questions the teacher can understand your reaction to what is being said. Communication is a two-way process. A dialogue develops between the one who teaches and those who are taught.

A *mass communications* industry has developed in the last hundred years. It is not just at school that we are educated. At home you learn informally as you read newspapers and magazines, when you listen to the radio and while you watch television or films at the cinema. These methods of communication play a part in your formal education at school because modern educational practices make use of audio-visual aids – learning through hearing and seeing. What parts of your education have been helped by films or filmstrips, cassettes or school broadcasting programmes?

Television is one of the most exciting innovations in our modern world. Sight is often the most effective of all the senses as a way of receiving information while hearing comes a close second. Television, combining the two, can be very influential. In Britain alone, as many as twenty million people may watch a TV programme. How do we know the number of people who watch particular TV programmes? One method used by *social research* investigators is *sampling*; interviewers go from door to door or stop people in the street and complete a *questionnaire* by asking them a set pattern of questions. One such *survey* indicated that women watch TV more than men. Children are subjected to an enormous variety of programmes.

In many ways television is of great benefit to society. It may help keep the family together at home. It is a help to old people and parents who stay at home because they cannot get baby sitters. Some programmes are very

'I'm a DON'T KNOW and my husband is a GET KNOTTED.'

educational while others provide entertainment for the whole family. Which television programmes do you consider especially informative?

In other ways television has been claimed to be a bad influence on people, especially on children. What programmes do you think could be included in that category? What sort

'Boy! It certainly wasn't suitable for children was it, Dad?'

64 INTRODUCING SOCIAL STUDIES

of people could be encouraged to commit crimes by seeing violence on television? Some people think that sex should not be shown on the television screen, because it encourages people to have bad morals. What sort of values do you think these people have in mind? Do you think that television sometimes strengthens people's *prejudices* (one-sided ideas), particularly about race? You may have watched *Till Death Us Do Part* or *Love Thy Neighbour*. Do these programmes make people laugh away their prejudices or do they harden people's attitudes towards members of other races?

Imagine that your television has broken down for a month. How do you think you would spend the time when you would otherwise have been watching television?

Although there are special TV programmes for schools, or for students studying for the Open University, all programmes may be considered as educational in some sense. Television and radio have three main uses:

1. to inform
2. to educate
3. to entertain.

'They want you to do a TV commercial on seat belts.

How would you try to separate these three aspects? When you listen to the news, you are being informed but you are being educated at the same time! Can you think of other ways in which you could be educated and entertained at the same time? Have you ever found that you learned more during a school lesson when the teacher made you laugh or amused you in some way?

What responsibilities have the Independent Broadcasting Authority or the British Broadcasting Corporation for programmes they broadcast? You probably know that the IBA controls commercial broadcasting whereas the BBC is a government body. Both of these authorities keep a careful watch over their programmes. Do you think they should give the public exactly what it wants, or should they introduce unusual things which people might not think they want but find they enjoy? The programmes have to cater for differences of outlook. Where a small proportion of people enjoy a pursuit we call this a *minority interest*; such an interest might become popular with the majority if they see enough of it.

Can you describe the general difference between programmes on BBC1 and BBC2? Can you think of any pursuits which have been popularised by exposing them to millions of people? What programmes would you like (a) more of, and (b) less of?

What answer would you give to people who say that so-called soap operas like *Coronation Street* and *Crossroads* are just time-wasters? One way to resolve the conflict of interests is to have special channels for different tastes. For example, Radio Four is a programme largely of talking, but Radio One offers almost continuous pop music.

Broadcasting – by radio and television – is only one way of communicating to the mass of the people. Another mass medium of communication is the press – newspapers,

COMMUNICATING 65

How advertising money is spent

periodicals, etc. Yet another medium is the cinema. (The plural of 'medium' is 'media'.)

We classify ways of communicating with millions of people as the *mass media*. Advertising must also be considered as part of the mass media business; people are influenced in making their purchases by *hidden persuaders*. The instruments of the mass media are used to inform consumers about goods on the market. The general public has a scarcity of spending money and the advertisers try to get them to spend it in a certain way. On the whole, newspapers concentrate on *informative advertising*, i.e. they communicate information about products, prices, performances, etc. Television is used more as a means of *persuasive advertising*. What things have the ad men been trying to persuade you to buy during the last week?

Contrary to general belief more money is spent on press advertising than on television advertising. Apart from about a dozen large national papers there are over 1000 local or specialised papers and journals. If it were not for the finance provided by advertisers you would be paying twice as much for your daily papers.

Newspapers can be divided into *popular papers* and *quality papers*. The figure shows the four main popular daily papers and four quality papers.

Most of these favour one of the main political parties and therefore have a certain bias. Have a look through the papers yourself and see which ones you think support Conservative or Labour or Liberal interests. The only communist paper is the *Morning Star*. It is part of your social education to find out the various prejudices of the newspapers which you read. Popular newspapers devote more space to human-interest stories than to political and economic news. Look at the photograph of the news-stand.

The flysheet does not reveal much. Perhaps some mysterious scandal and new shocks are on the way! What attitude does your daily paper take towards the trade unions or towards Northern Ireland? Try checking a particular newspaper story over a period of time. You may find newspapers contradict themselves or conveniently ignore items that figured prominently a few days ago. A social investigator must be careful in selecting *sources* of news. If an article bears the name of a prominent journalist or is from a news agency (such as Reuters or Associated Press), then more reliance can be placed upon it than on one which gives no source of origin.

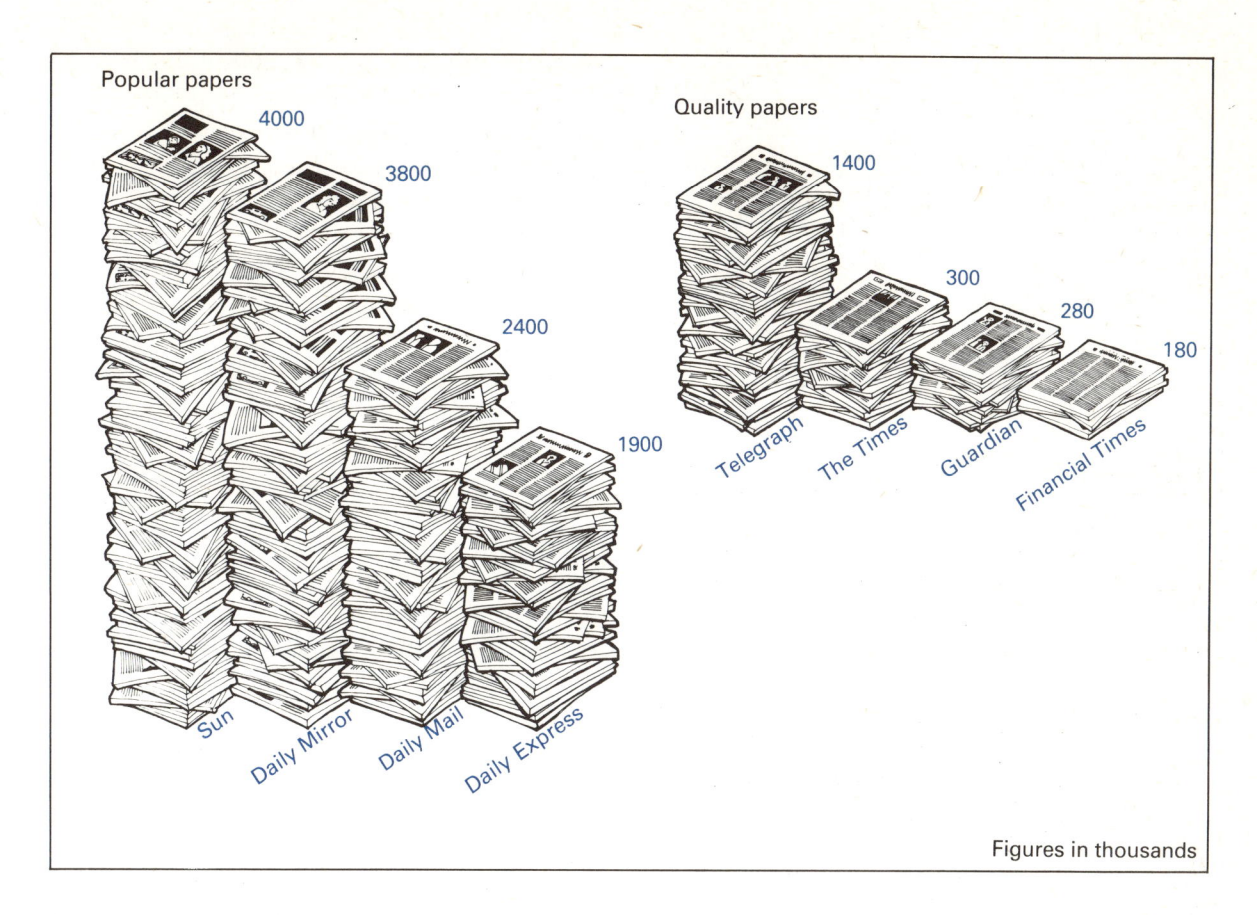

Popular papers — 4000, 3800, 2400, 1900
Sun, Daily Mirror, Daily Mail, Daily Express

Quality papers — 1400, 300, 280, 180
Telegraph, The Times, Guardian, Financial Times

Figures in thousands

The most frequently read daily papers

Is the most important news of the day always on the flysheet?

A newspaper has tremendous influence. There is always far more news than it is possible to print, so the power of selection is used. It is difficult for a reader to decide how much is news and how much is comment upon the news. Bold headlines can be misleading. It may be the newspaper's policy to attack an individual who is prominent in public life. An editor or leader writer has the power to influence *mass opinion*. The British buy more newspapers per head than any other nation on earth. The Scottish *Daily Record* alone is able to print 60 000 copies an hour.

Although films are shown on television and at the cinema, there are social differences between TV viewing and cinema-going. The cinema is one of the places where young

COMMUNICATING 67

Making up a page of the *Scottish Daily Record* – why is the man listening so carefully to the phone?

people can meet socially. Although the number of cinemas and cinema audiences have declined since the heyday of the movies thirty to forty years ago, there are still over two million cinema admissions in Britain every year. The film industry is fighting back by using larger screens, making expensive spectaculars and showing several feature films at one time in the new multi-cinemas. The film is a medium of communication which is sometimes entertaining, sometimes informative but always, in some way, educational.

Things to do and think about

1. Suggest some circumstances where you might wish to communicate by:
   (a) a frown
   (b) a smile
   (c) jumping for joy
   (d) clenching your fist
   (e) pointing your finger.
2. Collect pictures of pop groups. What kinds of message are they conveying?
3. What are the educational advantages of:
   (a) music and movement
   (b) drama
   (c) physical exercise?
4. Use your imagination to illustrate how we learn by first *observing*, and then *doing*, in:
   (a) individual situations
   (b) group situations
   (c) community situations.
5. By a group effort, produce a newspaper, covering:
   (a) recent news items about your school
   (b) a survey of your group's reading habits
   (c) advertisements appealing to: (i) safety, (ii) sex, (iii) speed
   (d) articles to: (i) inform, e.g. about cycling, (ii) entertain, e.g. about competitions, (iii) educate, e.g. about comprehensive education.

68 INTRODUCING SOCIAL STUDIES

6 By using a copy of the *Radio Times* and the *TV Times* make a survey of radio or television programmes during one week. The skeleton chart below will help you, but you will have to extend the programme groupings. Make a note of the number of hours given up to each type of programme.

serials   series   pop concerts   sports   crime

*Monday
Tuesday
Wednesday
Thursday
Friday
Saturday
Sunday*

7 Imagine you are a television interviewer. State which famous person you would most like to interview. What kinds of questions do you think you could ask to find out more about one person? Group the questions under headings, e.g. some under the heading 'beliefs', some under 'personality', etc.

8 What are your three favourite magazines? Why do you like them? In what ways could they be improved?

9 Choose a film which you have seen recently. In what ways did it:
   (a) give you a view of how people behave in an unusual situation;
   (b) provide escape from the reality (real-life society) you have experienced?

10 Invent some persuasive advertising headlines by adopting the technique of using the names of well-known television programmes.

Thus:

Coronation Street – a slice of life for the British tourist

or

Kojak lollies – suck one today

Terms used in Unit 4

social behaviour	non-verbal communication
culture	social interactions
non-industrial society	mass communications
industrial society	social research
methods of communication	sampling
traditional skills	questionnaire
cultural change	survey
exchange	prejudices
basic education	minority interest
informal education	mass media
formal education	hidden persuaders
knowledge	informative advertising
intelligence	persuasive advertising
equality of opportunity	popular papers
evidence	quality papers
experimental activity	sources
scarcity	mass opinion

COMMUNICATING 69

UNIT 5
You and your local community

TOPIC 5.1 Living in a community

A community is a group of people who share a common purpose. A *community spirit* is seen most clearly when people live together in a village, although it may also be found on a housing estate or even within a small area of a very large town.

You are interested in the people who live nearby – the people whom you see daily face-to-face. You know them as people; you know something of their interests, their characters, their relatives, their friends. They know you and recognise you as part of the community.

What boundaries would you draw round your community? If you live in a village you will probably find this easy. Look at the drawing of a village. Pick out the church, school, village hall and the pub. These are the *social centres* of community life. The houses cluster round them. You might expect to find a village green, a post office and a grocer's shop. What other things would you expect there to be in a village? Remember that a *village community* is likely to be made up of a few hundred people. As there is, on average, one policeman to every five hundred people in Britain, several small villages might have to share a policeman. Keeping the peace, or what we call formal social control, is easier in a village than in a town because almost everybody knows everybody else. If you do anything wrong in a village it is likely that people will soon find out. It is not easy for a law-breaker to hide in a rural community.

There are still some *traditional occupations* in the countryside. The shepherd in the photograph is looking after his sheep. His is a very specialised job.

Division of labour began with community living. Thousands of years ago people settled down to live in groups. You may have heard the Bible stories of how David looked after the sheep and that Jesus was a carpenter. In

A typical village

This is one of the oldest traditional occupations – what others can you think of?

medieval times people specialised in being wheelwrights or blacksmiths or tailors or cobblers. People began to *exchange* the value of their labour for other goods and money developed because of the problems of exchange, e.g. how many sheep would you expect to get for a cow?

Years ago communities were more self-sufficient and did not have to depend upon outsiders for essentials.

> The cottagers had to 'rough it', to dispense with softness, to put up with ugliness: but by their own skill and knowledge they forced the main part of their living out of the soil and the materials of their own neighbourhood. . . . Though I never saw the system in its completeness, I came here soon enough to find a few old people still partially living by it. These old people, fortunate in the possession of their own cottages and a little land, were keepers of pigs and donkeys, and even a few cows.
> GEORGE BOURNE, *Change in the Village*

LIVING IN A COMMUNITY

Bagging chickens before sending them off to be frozen or direct to the store

Convenience foods employ thousands in the numerous stages of getting the food to the buyer

You may be a member of more than one community. There is the community where you live and the community where you go to school or work.

Today many village-dwellers leave their homes every morning and go to work in a town. In cooperation with thousands of other people they work in an office or a store or a factory. How many people can you count helping to pack chickens? Their job is part of the division of labour. How many different types of goods can you count in the supermarket?

Cultural changes are always taking place as people adapt to new social and economic forces. Today people are more interdependent. The village or rural community could not live without the town. You need goods made in the town, such as bicycles or transistors, and you need services which are probably centred in the town – libraries, fire engines, ambulances, hospitals. Even the local

One of the essential but less pleasant tasks to be organised for the community as a whole

What precautions can people take to protect themselves from such pollution?

refuse collection is organised from the council offices situated in the town, and what a vital community service this is!

Town-dwellers also need the *country-dwellers*. Although only three per cent of British people work in farming, the agricultural industry supplies about half of the food we eat. The rest is imported. The village of Gosforth in Cumbria is typical:

> Over half the occupiers of farms who were farmers' sons themselves had worked as farm labourers at some time in their lives. The sons of farmers tend to be dependent on their fathers, whose instructions they follow in their work, and to whom they must go for pocket-money. But changes are taking place, for farms with a tractor tend to take their work pattern from the mechanically-minded son, because he can understand and work the tractor! Generally the father controls the finances and overall running of the farm, although the mother is responsible for the poultry and eggs, and keeps the money from these, and from the holiday-makers she may have as paying guests, for household goods and for clothes for the younger children. She may do her husband's accounts, and will help the men in the fields at busy times. . . .
>
> PAUL MATTHIAS, *Groups and Communities*

For over a century there has been a gradual movement of people from farming communities. This is part of the general *mobility of labour*, which means the movement of people from areas of underemployment to areas where work is available. The majority of people live in towns because they are employed there.

We have to be careful about man's modification of the environment. Modern communities pollute everything: the land, the water and the air.

Noise pollution is a form of air pollution; it is caused by the vibrations of the air around us. Noise pollution consists of unwanted or unpleasant sounds which annoy other members of the community. Noise is measured in decibels (dB) by a sound meter. The human

LIVING IN A COMMUNITY

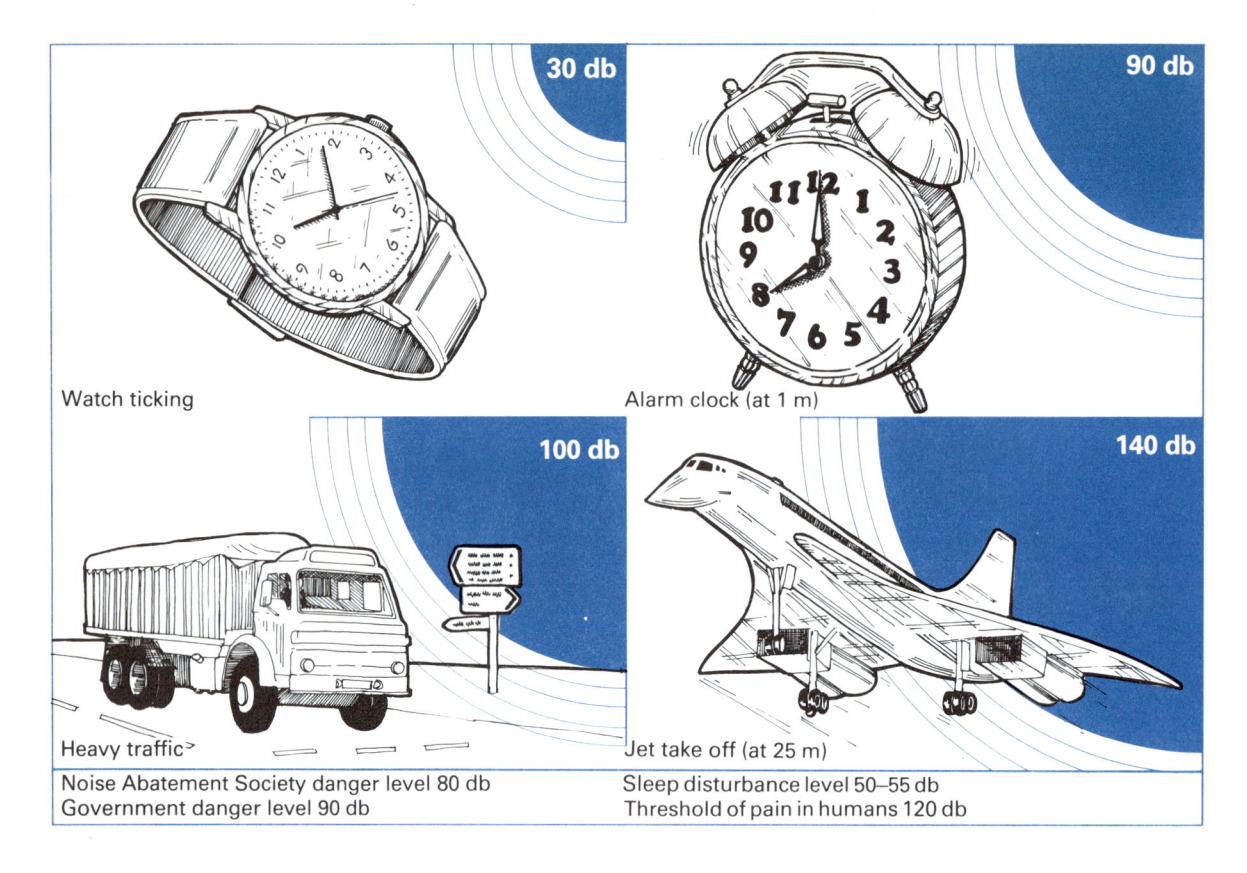

30 db Watch ticking	**90 db** Alarm clock (at 1 m)
100 db Heavy traffic	**140 db** Jet take off (at 25 m)
Noise Abatement Society danger level 80 db Government danger level 90 db	Sleep disturbance level 50–55 db Threshold of pain in humans 120 db

Noise pollution – which figures surprise you?

ear can just pick up a sound of 1 dB, whereas a space rocket may record a sound of 200 dB. The aircraft shown on page 73 is likely to be responsible for a noise of well over 100 dB. The sound threshold of pain for human beings is about 120 dB. A modern jet aircraft would record about 150 dB at a distance of twenty-five metres.

We know that as individuals we show marked differences. What is considered loud by one person might be thought reasonable by another. Young people who enjoy discos think older people are spoilsports when they tell their children that they may become the deaf generation. A disco is likely to 'score' about 120 dB. The government considers anything more than 90 dB is harmful; 80 dB is reckoned as a damaging noise by the Noise Abatement Society. How much should we tolerate? This is one of the conflicts of modern community life. Although you may like noise, it is a fact that it may permanently harm your hearing. An *addict* is an individual who has a harmful habit which he cannot break. When a noise-addict becomes partially deaf, he demands higher noise-levels which are more harmful to him and his friends. One thing leads to another. Remember our concept of causality? (See page 17.)

Air pollution takes place when unpleasant substances are added to normal air. You probably know that normal air contains about one-fifth of oxygen, four-fifths of nitrogen, water vapour and other gases, including a little carbon dioxide which is necessary for plants and other growth. One of the worst

Congestion at the Carrow Road lifting bridge, Norwich

'I'm from downstairs. Your bathwater is coming through my ceiling.'

Unprotected waterways can be a hazard

forms of air pollution in a modern community is caused by carbon monoxide from the exhausts of motor vehicles. A conflict exists between those who want relatively cheap motoring and those who want clean air in the community. Do you think modern communities give up too much for the convenience of motorists? How many vehicles can you count in the photograph?

Community living depends upon cooperation and mutual dependence.

No man is an island.
    JOHN DONNE

An individual who smokes cigarettes is responsible for a most dangerous source of air pollution both to himself and to the community of which he is a member. Should an individual be able to do as he likes about smoking or has he any responsibility to the community?

Water pollution is found in seas, rivers, lakes and canals. They are made dirty by household sewage and factory waste. Have you ever seen a beach spoiled by oil? Or have you smelt a disused canal? What do you think would have happened to the little girl shown in the photograph if the policeman had not been there?

LIVING IN A COMMUNITY 75

Nuclear experts give warning on build-up of untreated waste fuel

From Roger Vielvoye
Vienna, May 24

Eight thousand tonnes of ... fuel with ... ponds throughout Europe by 1895 unless new facilities are built to recycle these materials.

A warning about the build-up of untreated irradiated nuclear fuel comes ... a group of sented to a conference of senior executives of Europe's electricity producers this week.

Shortage of reprocessing facilities could also become a bottle...

CYANIDE SCARE OVER

Relief surged through the village of Throgmorton when a small boy found the missing cannister of cyanide, which had fallen from a farmer's Land-... ten days ... Stephe...

WATER POLLUTION SCARE IS OVER

THE WATER contamination scare in Cambridgeshire was over for the time being, the Anglian Water Authority said today. Supplies were cut off yesterday to thousands of homes and busine... premises ...

Air noise 'increases mental illness'

By John Groser
Consumer Affairs Correspondent

evidence on the medi... particularly its effects on children, is to be presented to the Government. The Federation of Heathrow Anti-Noise has writt... M... ll, asking him urgently to examine the evidence and to take action.

The federation includes the Local Authorities (Aircraft Noise) Coun... nd the Noise Abateme...

We must all do our best to look after the countryside. We call this *conservation*. If the people of any community upset the balance of nature they do so at their peril. Can you think of any dangers in using chemical fertilisers or insecticides?

Can you think of the dangers of dropping litter carelessly in the country? What harm can be done by throwing away old bottles and empty fizzy drink cans?

The need for conservation often arises because human communities spoil the environment thus causing *pollution*. Vance Packard in *The Waste Makers* describes how many people do not bother to dispose carefully of their waste material. We litter our environment with domestic and industrial waste which we could dispose of, if only we took the trouble.

In 1976, Professor Richard Hoggart de-

76 INTRODUCING SOCIAL STUDIES

Although it is possible to recycle waste, collecting it can create more rubbish and a health hazard

A purpose-built home for the aged, but for whose convenience was it built?

Why does this home seem better than the other one?

scribed the British as the scruffiest nation in Europe. What can you and I do about it? Could your school arrange an anti-waste project?

A community must look after those who cannot look after themselves. Although we pride ourselves on our welfare services many people who need help do not get it. The mother-to-be gets help from social workers at a clinic. The young mother can take her baby to a clinic for regular check-ups, while a health visitor will visit the home to see that everything is all right. But although these facilities are freely available to all, many women do not take advantage of them, e.g. the immigrants who do not understand English, or deprived families. We need to be educated in how to use these services.

Old people need comfort and companionship. Look at the old ladies in the first picture and compare them with the group in the second.

Do you think the young and old have cheered each other up? Why is there sometimes less of a generation gap between the very young and the very old, than between teenagers and the older generation?

The old who are still independent in the community should not be forgotten until there is an emergency

Some old people do not want to live in a home. They have an independent spirit and want to try to manage on their own. But they are still the responsibility of the community which they once served. Look carefully at the old man in the armchair. Why does he need help quickly?

Things to do and think about

1. Draw simple plans of:
   (a) a village of long ago – you could include a manor house, common land, blacksmith's forge, village pump, etc.
   (b) a modern village – what may have happened to the manor house, common land, forge, etc.?
2. State whether you think the following statements are mostly true or untrue and give your reasons:
   (a) There is less snobbery in a village than in a town.
   (b) Community life is ruined because so many villagers commute to town to work.
   (c) Villagers are rarely vandals.
   (d) Most villages are just dormitory suburbs.
3. Make a plan for the improved development of your neighbourhood. Show changes you would make in roads, housing and other community services.
4. Write a short humorous poem called *Things are a-changing*.
5. The following words are about the pollution of a community's environment. Rearrange them into related pairs, e.g. exhaust fumes – carbon monoxide.

exhaust fumes	urban fog
cleaner air	nuclear power
burning waste	dead fish
litter	carbon monoxide
radiation	incinerators
smog	over 120 dB
oil slicks	cigarettes
coal tar	smokeless zones
Concorde	waste-bins

   Discuss your answers: there may be alternatives!
6. Use your library to find out about:
   (a) The Clean Air Acts of 1956 and 1968
   (b) The Nuclear Test Ban Treaty of 1963
   (c) The Merchant Shipping (Oil Pollution) Act of 1971
   (d) The Deposit of Poisonous Waste Act of 1972.
7. Find some press-cuttings about vandals. What factors do you think contribute to vandalism in your community?
8. Find out what things a parish council can do on behalf of a village community.
9. Draw a picture to illustrate *one* of the following:
   (a) a farming community
   (b) an industrial community
   (c) a commuting community
   (d) a community centre
   (e) a community of the future.
10. Suggest ways in which you could do some social service for your community.

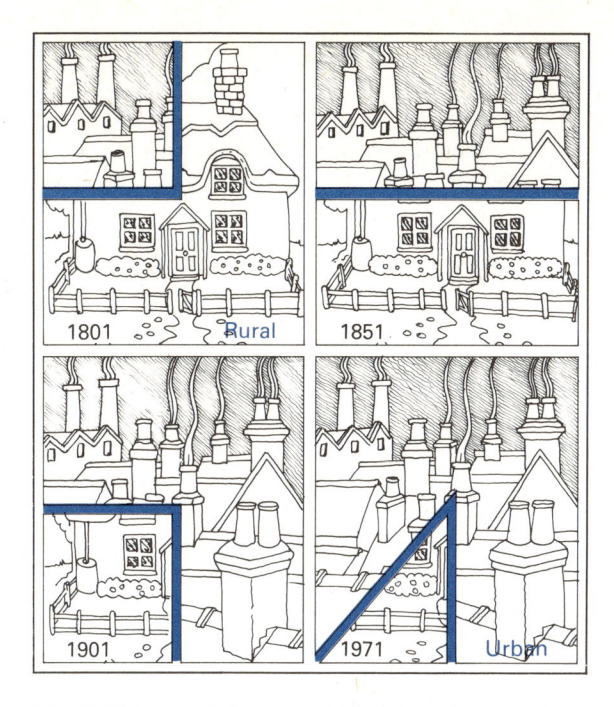

The British population has shifted from the country to the towns

TOPIC 5.2 Towns

You are more likely to live in a town or city than in the country. More than three-quarters of the people in Britain live in an *urban community*. As industrialisation has increased, the average British person has become a town-dweller rather than a country-dweller. This has led to overcrowding in the towns.

In addition to this movement of people, the population continues increasing. It is estimated that there will be about 60 million people in the United Kingdom by the year AD 2000 and that about 50 million of them will live in towns. The growth in population may be less than estimated because the *birth rate* (the number of live births per 1000 people) is declining. However, the number already born, combined with the fact that people now live longer, will result in an increasing population for some years yet.

The growth of towns forces people to live

Shore Road may no longer exist but many families still live in houses without bathrooms or hot water, etc.

more crowded lives. Look at the scene in London's Shore Road in 1943.

Crowded areas are likely to result in **slum** dwellings. A *slum* is a place which is unfit for human habitation. In Britain today there are still over a million homes which ought to be demolished and the families rehoused. An organisation called Shelter draws attention to bad housing. It is what we call a *pressure group* – a group of people who are very concerned about a particular problem and struggle to get something done about it.

The lower photograph, taken on behalf of

TOWNS 79

Shelter, shows life in a poor area of a big town. This is known as a 'grey area' or *twilight zone*. The housing is inadequate by our modern standards but there are far worse places. The spirit of community may be strong in twilight areas and people may stick together to help each other. This zone is usually not far from the city centre and is made up mainly of old houses awaiting demolition, but with some good housing as well.

There are several types of dwelling in which we can live. A terraced, semi-detached or detached house; a high-rise flat; a maisonette; a bungalow. Over half of the houses or flats in Britain may be grouped or *classified* as 'owner-occupier' houses, inhabited by people who are buying their own houses over a period of twenty to thirty years.

About a third of those in towns rent council houses. Some excellent houses have been built by local authorities, especially in recent years. The photograph shows houses built at South Dorcan, Swindon, in the early 1970s. They have been especially planned to allow people to live without being troubled by motor vehicles. Towns are places for living in. They should be designed for people rather than for cars.

Of course people who live in towns want to own motor vehicles. Apart from having a car or motorcycle for private use, town-dwellers need a good transport system to take them about their daily business and for the delivery of goods and mail.

Public transport is becoming more important as towns are so crowded. Work out roughly how many people could be transported in the buses shown in the photograph. How many cars would be needed to carry all those people if they journeyed two persons to a car?

In Britain there is a network of towns linked by road and rail communications. Our interdependence means that one town depends

80 INTRODUCING SOCIAL STUDIES

Housing stock by tenure – who owns the property you live in?

A modern 'people first' housing estate

Why is the postman such an important person in the community?

Public transport is a necessary service but not only *within* towns

The new high speed train saves time, reduces road traffic yet railways are still cutting services – why?

upon another for the satisfaction of its needs. Most of our road traffic is privately owned but the railway system is nationalised; that is, owned by the state. Inter-city rail traffic is one of the most important forms of public transport. People are whisked speedily from one large city to another without having to face overcrowded road traffic which we call *congestion*. Above right you can see one of the latest trains which can travel at well over 160 km/h. The driver of this locomotive would not have to waste time by being required to stop at traffic lights or by a police officer on point duty. Good rail transport is needed to carry passengers and heavy goods between towns; community life within the town itself would not be possible nowadays without smooth-flowing road traffic.

In large towns it is essential to have certain people in authority. The traffic warden in the picture has authority over the drivers of vehicles in one part of London. Over seven million people live in London. As there are about 56 million people in the United Kingdom one out of every eight Britons lives

A traffic warden in a familiar role – what other duties do wardens have?

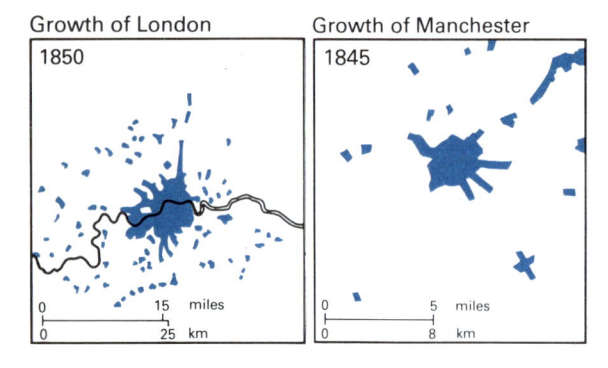

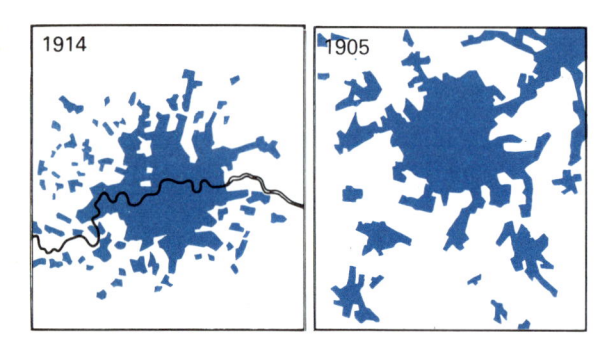

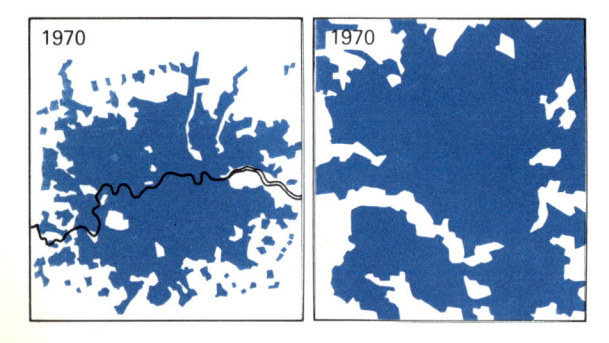

Growth of London — 1850, 1914, 1970
Growth of Manchester — 1845, 1905, 1970

Conurbations grow in different ways — compare London and Manchester

in this enormous town. It is the capital or metropolis and largest community in the country. Within the Greater London area there are many boroughs. They are urban communities within the larger community of the metropolis. London is by far the largest town in Britain but there are other large conurbations. A *conurbation* is a very large town formed by smaller towns gradually joining together. Glasgow, with a population of over 800 000 is the only conurbation in Scotland. Other conurbations are shown in the table below. Since local government was reorganised in 1974, these huge urban areas have been under the authority of newly-formed metropolitan counties.

metropolitan counties	*largest towns*
Merseyside	Liverpool
South East Lancashire	Manchester
West Midlands	Birmingham
Tyne and Wear	Newcastle
West Yorkshire	Leeds
South Yorkshire	Bradford

Birmingham has a population of just over one million and is the largest conurbation outside London.

About one-third of the people of Britain live in the conurbations and nearly half live in smaller towns.

Some interesting changes in town life have taken place in the *New Towns*. These have been set up under the New Towns Act, 1946, which was intended to combat overcrowded conditions found in very large towns. Some of these new towns include Milton Keynes, Cumbernauld, East Kilbride, Livingstone, Washington, Telford, Harlow, Basildon, Bracknell and Crawley. Milton Keynes started its life in 1967 and will one day have a population of over a quarter of a million people. A new town gives town-planners a chance to start afresh and design a town without too many conflicts with traditional

INTRODUCING SOCIAL STUDIES

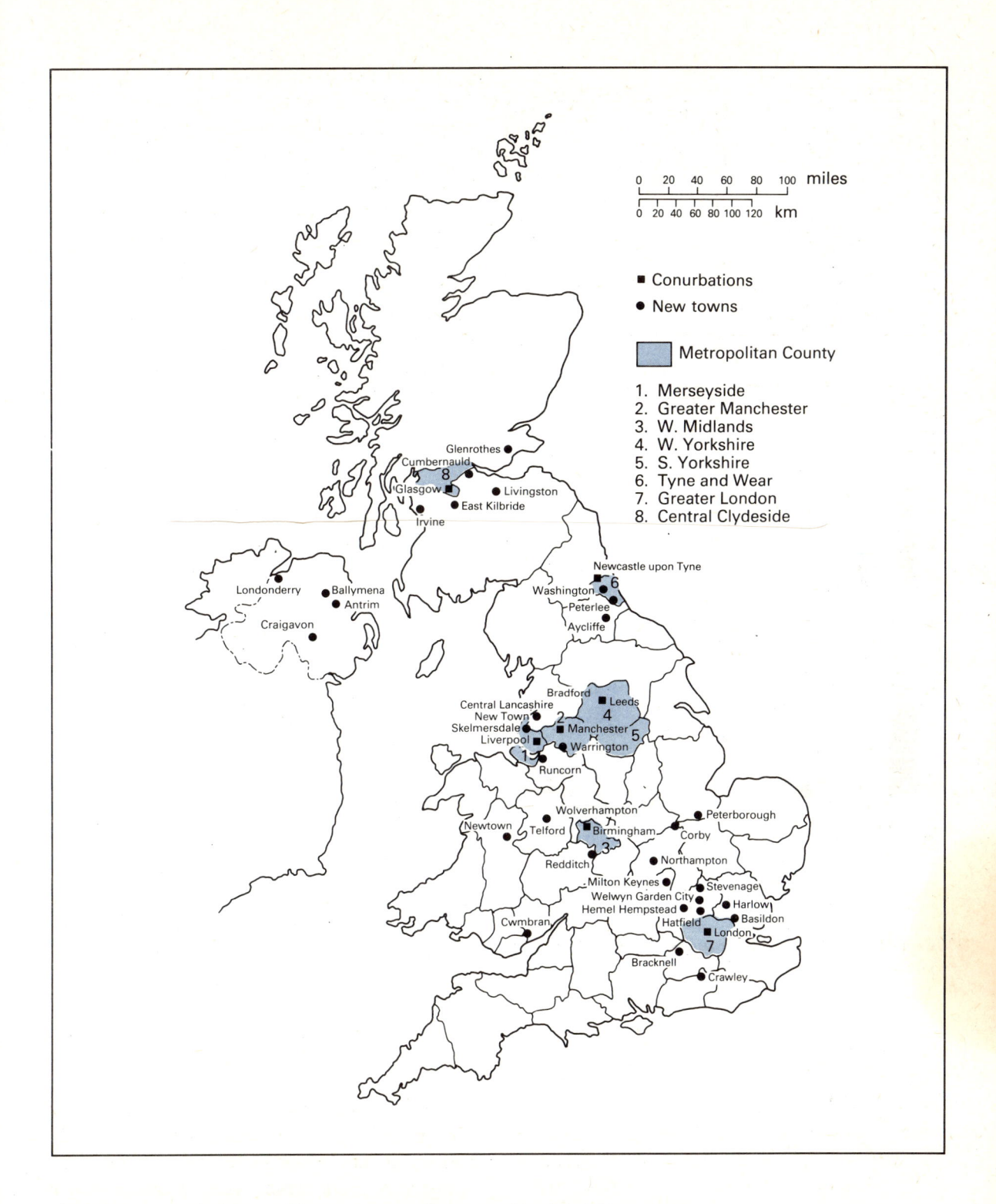

New towns, conurbations and the new metropolitan counties of the UK

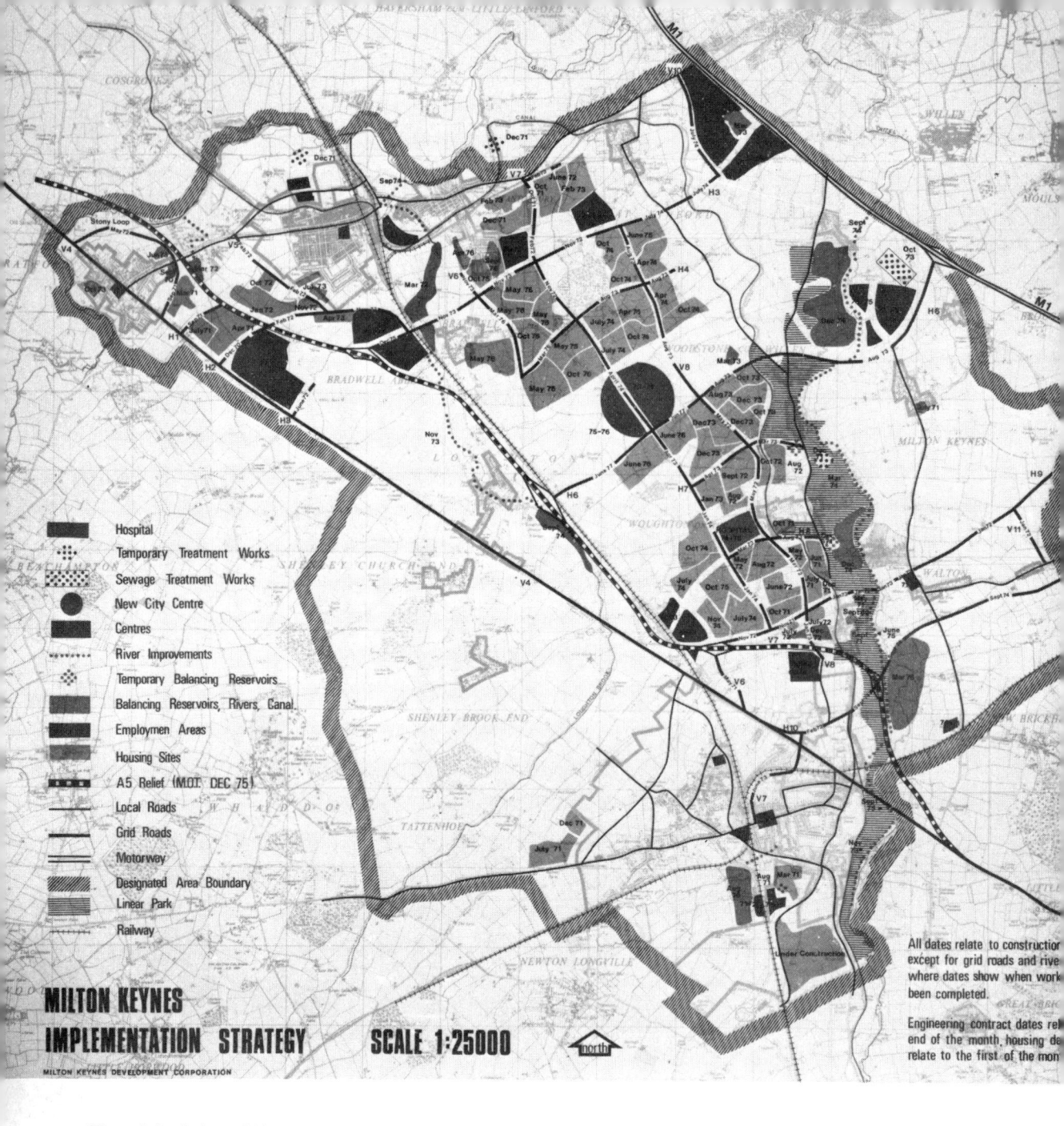

The original plan of Milton Keynes

interests. There will always be some conflicts because even a new town has to be sited where some people are already living!

Expansion schemes have been used to breathe new life into some medium-sized towns steeped in old traditions. Other smaller places such as Thetford, in Norfolk, have been classified as *overspill towns*; new houses and factories have been built and the towns much enlarged by an influx of newcomers. What advantages and disadvantages are these newcomers likely to experience?

Those who live in towns enjoy many benefits. There will be a choice of shops and sporting facilities, banks and building societies, museums and libraries, churches and cinemas, restaurants and hotels, and a hundred and one other things which those who live in the countryside find in scarce supply. The centres of many large towns have been much improved in recent years with *shopping precincts* for pedestrians.

On the other hand town-dwellers have to pay high rates to the local government authority. All the extra services of street lighting, well-paved roads, schools, art galleries, traffic control, etc., have to be paid for by the ratepayers and taxpayers.

Many town-dwellers live in the *suburbs* or outskirts of large towns. They may lack a *social nucleus* or centre of community life. Their living area is a dormitory suburb. Their main interests may lie elsewhere, such as in the town centre.

People who live in towns surrounded by *green belts*, upon which no further building is allowed, have a chance to breathe cleaner air than is found in industrial areas. The green belts are the lungs of the city. People who are unable to enjoy living in the countryside itself, can at least enjoy the fresh air of parks and recreation grounds, and the green spaces which separate one town from another. We must conserve our environment for the sake of those who live in the community and on behalf of the people who are yet to come.

Things to do and think about

1 Devise your own key and make a plan of an urban area (preferably in your own town) indicating places you consider vital to community life, for example:
schools and colleges (E = education)
shops and stores
churches and chapels
hospitals and clinics
doctors' and dentists' surgeries
libraries, museums and art galleries
community centres, youth clubs and old people's homes
police and fire stations
discotheques, soccer grounds, bingo halls and pubs
recreation and play grounds.
Which of those marked on your map does your family use?

2 Read the following account about gypsies.

Estimates of the number of travelling families in England and Wales at the end of 1974 vary from 4500 to about 8000. If we accept the higher estimate, which is probably nearer the truth since it is based on field workers' reports, only 21 per cent of families had been provided with either a permanent or temporary site at this date. Whatever the actual figure, the lack of sites

Why do people object to providing sites for gypsies?

TOWNS 85

is generally deplored by people working with gypsies in an advocacy role, and local authorities are being urged, by the Gypsy Council, for example, to act more quickly in establishing sites. Conversations with travellers suggest that many do want to live on sites, which is an understandable preference since the alternative is to camp by the roadside, with the risk of prosecution under the 1959 Highways Act, or to trespass on land, with the likelihood of harassment and eviction. The choice is often between residence on a site or a permanent state of insecurity.

DAVID SIBLEY, 'The provision of sites for gypsies,' *The Planner, Journal of the Royal Town Planning Institute*, Vol. 62, May 1976

What would you do to give gypsies more security for temporary visits and for permanent residence?

3 Pair the names and drawings shown below:

detached houses	bungalows
semi-detached houses	chalets
terraces	high-rise flats
town houses	prefabs

4 Make a list of goods which might be bought by your family as the weekly 'groceries'. Carry out a survey, and make a comparison between the prices charged for these items at:
(a) a corner shop
(b) a large store
(c) a local market
(d) a supermarket.

5 On squared paper make a plan of an ideal new town. Begin by drawing in a river, the main roads and railway. The number of squares you use for each item will depend on your own opinion of its importance to the community, for example:

item	square guide
infant or first schools	$\frac{1}{2}$
middle schools	1
secondary schools	$1\frac{1}{2}$
technical college	2
bus station	2
railway station	$2\frac{1}{2}$
sewage works	3

Now carry on with twenty items of your own choice.

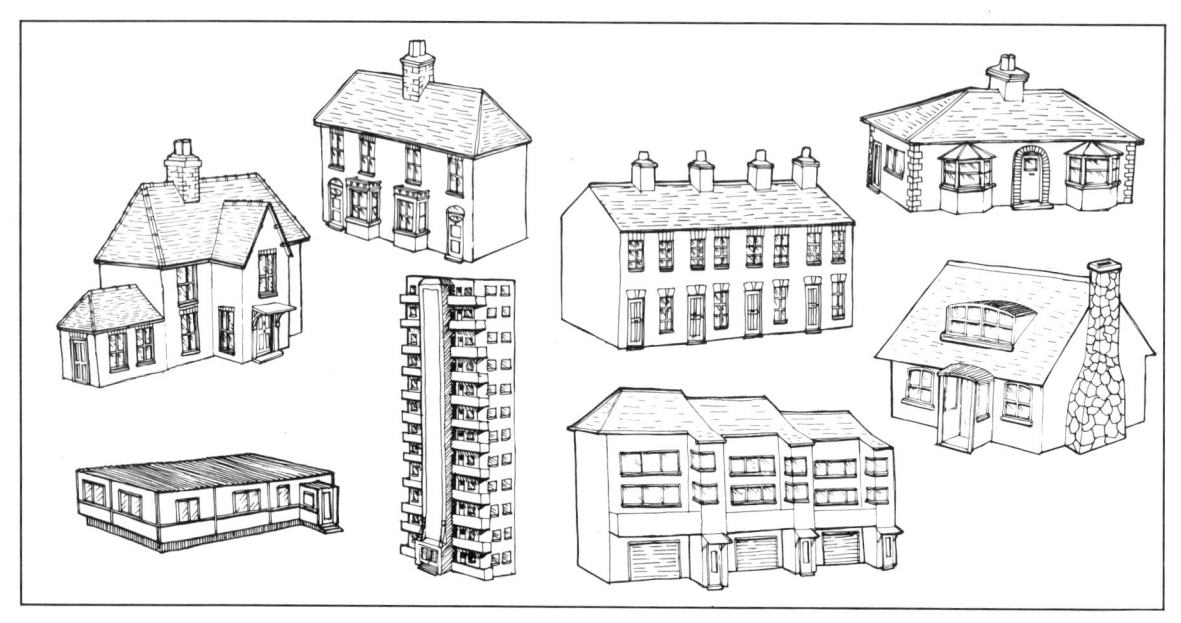

6 Do some research on *one* of the following in preparation for a short talk that you are to give to your group:
  (a) Community Service Volunteers
  (b) The Carnegie Trust
  (c) The Nuffield Foundation
  (d) The Civic Trust.

7 Trace a rough outline map of the UK from an atlas and mark on it ten of the following towns and cities. Mark them with dots varying in size according to their different populations given below in thousands:

town	*population*
London	7281
Birmingham	1004
Glasgow	836
Liverpool	575
Manchester	531
Sheffield	512
Leeds	500
Edinburgh	449
Bristol	422
Belfast	354
Coventry	334
Nottingham	295
Cardiff	277
Wolverhampton	270
Stoke	260
Dundee	181
Aberdeen	181

8 See if you can obtain a copy of a rate demand. On this you will see listed the items on which the council spends the ratepayer's money. List them in order, with the one costing the most at the top of the list. Would you change the order?

What problems can this man have when using town amenities? (See question 9.)

9 How could town amenities be made easier for disabled people to use?

Terms used in Unit 5

community spirit
social centres
village community
traditional occupations
exchange
town-dwellers
country-dwellers
mobility of labour
addict
conservation
pollution
urban community
birth rate

slum
pressure group
twilight zone
classified
congestion
conurbation
New Towns
expansion schemes
overspill towns
shopping precincts
suburbs
social nucleus
green belts

TOWNS 87

UNIT 6
Living in our national community

TOPIC 6.1 What is a national community?

You are a member of a national community as well as of a local community. Although members of a national community have their differences as individuals they have particular features or *characteristics* which they share.

What things unite or join us into a national community? We speak the same language, use the same coinage and postage stamps, recognise the Union Jack as our national flag. What other unifying things can you think of?

There are things which most of us do, although some members of our national community might not believe in them: we pride ourselves on freedom of speech although there may be a few people who hold extreme views. The majority recognise the Queen as monarch but there are some Britons who might prefer a republic with a president as head of state.

Although we live in a national community we do not force people into one way of living. We respect each other's differences. There is a lot of conflict but also a lot of cooperation between politicians. We are free to support any religion, or no religion at all.

There are some things which we expect of all those who live in our national community: we expect them to obey the law of the land. There are other things which are considered typically British but which few people do

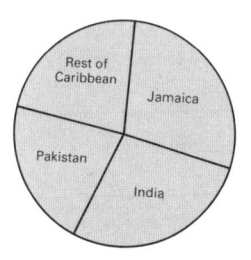

Where most of our New Commonwealth immigrants come from

A Salvation Army band practising – where and when do you see them most often in action?

nowadays. These are customs based on our tradition. How many times have you seen Morris dancing, or a maypole, or the Boat Race, or a Punch and Judy show? Yet these are considered typically British because they are not usually associated with the customs and traditions of other national communities.

All groups have their sense of values and their members share similar ideas, beliefs and associations. This is true in a general way of a national group. We talk of the British sense of fair play, and pride ourselves on being sportsmen. Do you think our image in this respect has been spoiled in recent years because of the activities of football supporters? What can we do to improve our image?

We saw in the first unit that the British community is made up of people who have come to live here from all over the world. It is a multi-cultural community. Some came to conquer: Romans from Italy, Saxons from Germany, Vikings from Scandinavia and Normans from France. Others came in peace: refugees from religious persecution for many centuries, and refugees from fascism and communism in the twentieth century.

Since the Second World War, many *immigrants* from the New Commonwealth (for example, India, Pakistan and the West Indies) have come to live in this country.

An immigrant bus conductor – a common sight in our big cities

The majority of immigrants become a less privileged class in Britain and many have to take jobs that others do not want, such as working on the tube trains in London and on the buses. But some take professional jobs and become doctors, nurses, engineers and accountants. Our transport and health services would break down without their help. By the mid-seventies nearly two million (or about 3 per cent) of our people were coloured.

There are a number of minority groups within our national community. There are class minorities, e.g. the aristocracy and the rich; and there are *ethnic* minorities, e.g. Jews, Indians. The rich tend to live in certain expensive parts of cities and in the 'stockbroker belt'. Coloured people have also tended to settle in certain neighbourhoods, especially in such places as London, Bradford and Wolverhampton. The photograph shows

WHAT IS A NATIONAL COMMUNITY

Muslims preserving part of their own culture in Britain

A typical demonstration

members of a Muslim community taking part at a music session at Brentford in London. Can you pick the odd man out? Perhaps he is trying to understand this music which is part of these people's heritage or culture.

We have seen throughout this book that there will always be conflicts to settle. There is now a law in this country making it compulsory for those riding on motorcycles to wear crash helmets. The law was designed to save lives but caused a problem for Sikh members of the community because it is one of their religious beliefs that they must wear turbans. It is part of their tradition. Mohan Hartung Singh of Bedford was the first Sikh to be charged in Britain because he insisted on wearing a turban rather than a crash helmet. By 1973 he had been before the courts over twenty times. In the end he won his case.

Mohan Hartung Singh's sincere beliefs caused him to engage in an individual conflict against authority. Other racial differences lead to more serious consequences especially when people have prejudices which make them unwilling to *integrate* or become part of a multi-racial community. In 1976 a coloured youth was murdered during disturbances in the London borough of Southall. Of the five youths charged with his murder, one was coloured. Demonstrations followed throughout London and a few days later a white youth died from stab wounds after a fight involving two Asians and a number of white youths. This is an example of how *racial tension* builds up. Think of some reasons for racial tension building up, e.g. poverty, unequal opportunity.

In Britain there is a tradition of allowing individuals *freedom* of thought, speech, word and movement. People can organise protest groups and demonstrations if they wish. In this picture Greek Cypriots are demonstrating in London.

In some countries the authorities themselves put on demonstrations, in others they ban them and in others they allow any group to demonstrate peacefully. It is an essential part of life in our national community that all our people should be free to air their views so long as they grant other people the same right.

Things to do and think about

1 Pick two national communities and compare their:
 (a) style of dress
 (b) food
 (c) customs
 (d) manners.

2. The British speak a Germanic language closely resembling Danish, Dutch and German. See if you can complete the gaps in the table. (Here is a clue: they all involve family relationships.)

Danish	*Dutch*	*German*	*English*
Fader	Vader	Vater	?
Moder	Moeder	Mutter	?
Broder	Broeder	Bruder	?
Søster	Zuster	Schwester	?
Søn	Zoon	Sohn	?
Datter	Dochter	Tochter	?

3. (a) Draw a strip cartoon illustrating British national customs and festivals not mentioned in the text, for example:
 (i) London to Brighton veteran car race
 (ii) Pancakes on Shrove Tuesday
 (iii) Carol singing
 (iv) The Grand National.
 (b) What do you associate with:
 (i) Valentine's Day
 (ii) Remembrance Day
 (iii) Easter Sunday
 (iv) Guy Fawkes's Day
 (v) Christmas Day?

4. What did Voltaire mean when he wrote this?
 > I loathe what you say, I disagree with all of it, and I will fight to the death for your right to say it.

5. Imagine you are explaining the British way of life to a foreigner who has recently come to this country. How would you describe our:
 (a) clothes (d) houses
 (b) food   (e) humour
 (c) holidays (f) music?

6. In what ways are the British people changing in their
 (a) leisure and recreation habits
 (b) living conditions (including furniture)
 (c) shopping habits
 (d) use of Sundays?

TOPIC 6.2 Our government and the law

Have you ever been to the House of Commons? Look at the picture. The most important members of the *Government* of the day sit to the Speaker's right. The Speaker is the man in the wig who is on the extreme right of the picture. He is Chairman of the House of Commons. In front of him are three clerks, then there is the large table upon which official papers are laid, and then the mace and the Sergeant-at-Arms. The mace is the *symbol* of authority and is always there when the House is sitting. About twenty of the most important members of the government form the

The House of Commons in session

Cabinet. These are ministers in charge of government departments such as the Foreign Office, the Home Office, education, employment, health and social security.

On the opposite side of the illustration you will see the Shadow Cabinet. They are members of the *Opposition* who are likely to form the Cabinet if their party wins the next general election and comes to power. They are picked by the Leader of the Opposition who is paid a salary in addition to that of the ordinary MPs to oppose the government. It is an interesting aspect of our *democracy* that we pay this salary to someone who has the job of opposing the government and keeping it on its toes. A democracy is a government elected by the people.

How do 'the people' rule and exert their power and authority? General elections are held at least every five years and every person over the age of eighteen (except criminals, peers and lunatics) has the privilege of voting. Since 1872 we have voted by *secret ballot* so nobody knows how we vote unless we wish to tell them. We vote the way we want to and no one is allowed to pay money to get people to vote for them.

The majority of people vote for a candidate who represents one of the three major parties: Conservative, Liberal or Labour. The party which wins a majority of the 635 *constituencies* (electoral districts) becomes the Government of the day. The Queen calls upon the leader of that party to form a government; he or she becomes Prime Minister and chooses a Cabinet. The Prime Minister will want one of the party's best people to become Chancellor of the Exchequer and look after the nation's finances.

Parliament passes laws which are introduced by the government. A new law starts off as a bill which has to be passed by both the House of Commons and the House of Lords. The elected representatives of the people, i.e.

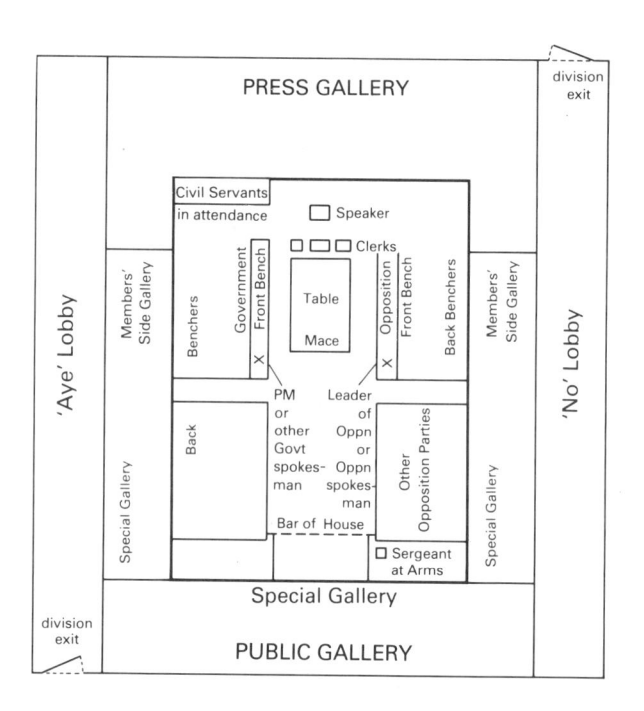

A simplified plan of the House of Commons

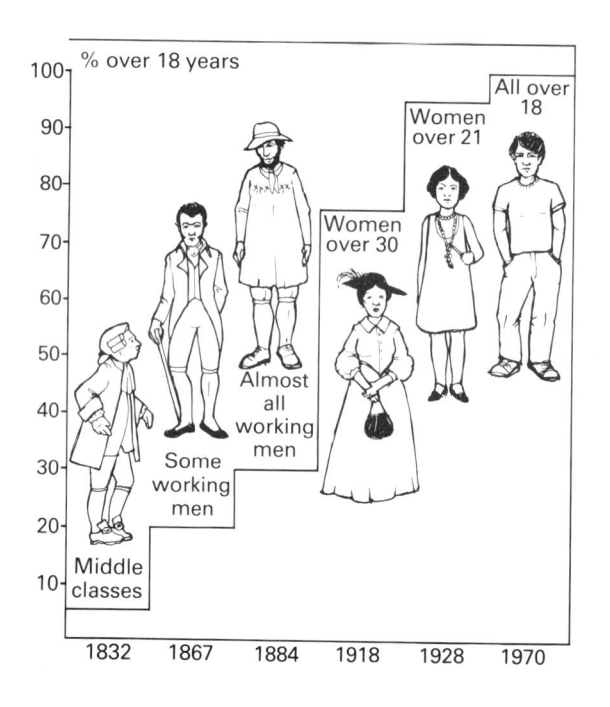

When people got the vote

92 INTRODUCING SOCIAL STUDIES

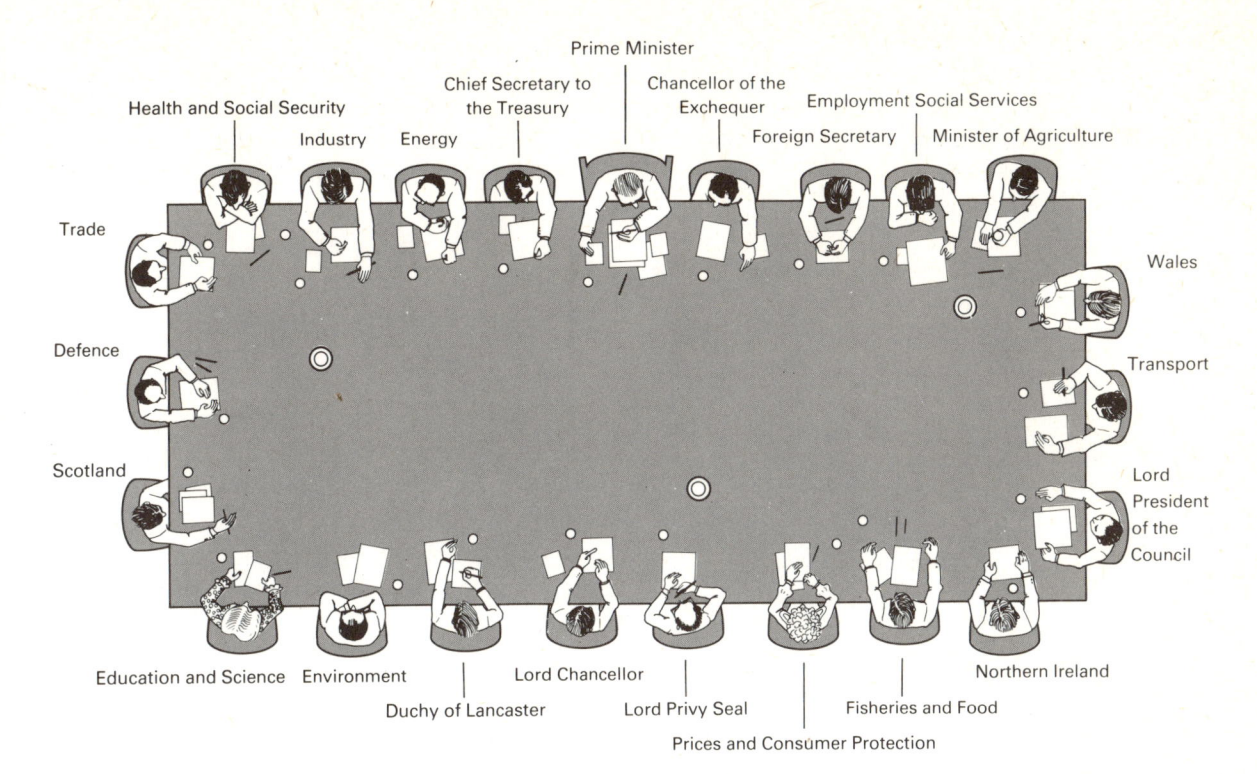

Members of the Cabinet

Cabinet positions labeled around table: Health and Social Security, Industry, Energy, Chief Secretary to the Treasury, Prime Minister, Chancellor of the Exchequer, Foreign Secretary, Employment Social Services, Minister of Agriculture, Wales, Transport, Lord President of the Council, Northern Ireland, Fisheries and Food, Prices and Consumer Protection, Lord Privy Seal, Lord Chancellor, Duchy of Lancaster, Environment, Education and Science, Scotland, Defence, Trade

the MPs, sit in the Commons. The Lords are not elected by the people. When a bill has been amended and agreed by both Houses of Parliament and has received the Royal Assent, it becomes an Act.

Every Act of Parliament becomes part of the law of our society. The police and the courts have the task of seeing that the law is kept. Apart from laws passed by Parliament there is:

(a) *common law* or rules accepted by tradition and now forming part of the law of the land;

(b) *case law* or decisions made by judges and used as yardsticks when considering similar cases.

The main *courts* are Magistrates' Courts where unpaid Justices of the Peace deal with about 98 per cent of all those who break the law. More serious crimes are dealt with by

Inside a juvenile court: the accused stands in the box beside the court usher who holds the Bible and explains the court proceedings – at the back sit 3 magistrates – down the side are the clerk of the court, a counsel and a social worker – the other man is an official

OUR GOVERNMENT AND THE LAW 93

'You heard me, I said no standing on top.'

higher courts such as Crown Courts where cases are tried by a judge and jury.

It is important that courts get to the truth and that justice is seen to be done. All those who give evidence have to take an oath which is a promise to tell the truth. Any person telling a lie on oath is guilty of the crime of *perjury*.

It is the responsibility of all members of our national community to keep the law and to see that the law is kept. A society must exercise some formal social control over its members even though this control limits people's freedom. By tradition we accept certain patterns of behaviour as reasonable; most people obey the law of the land because it is just and fair, and because we have been socialised into accepting it.

When people do break the law something has to be done about it. If law and order were

FIRE DAMAGE — £2 MILLION

Gardens trampled by fans on the rampage

MISSING CHILD FOUND IN SHALLOW GRAVE

Fighting breaks out among demonstrators

Shoplifting figures soar

Heavier penalties urged for motorists

to break down completely we would have chaos and no organised government. This is known as *anarchy*.

Why do some people break the law? Some do it unwittingly like leaving their cars for too long at parking meters. But we are concerned here with the more serious crimes and, as we have already seen when discussing the concept of causality, there is not one simple reason.

A higher percentage of people from poor housing than from adequate housing commit crimes; these people tend to have had unhappy childhoods, and do not have the opportunities to direct their energies into rewarding activities. They may also do jobs which are unskilled and boring. In crime they find 'kicks' to replace boredom, and feel they are being heroic. Or they may not be able to live in harmony with others because they did not learn from their parents how to live happily when they were children.

In this way they do not become adjusted to the society in which they live and suffer under the tensions this conflict produces. They join groups of people similar to themselves and live according to the norms of other deviants within the group. These norms become more important than the norms of the non-criminal society and exert powerful influence. The people may turn to violence, drug addiction, alcoholism, theft, etc.

A few people break the law over questions of conscience or *principle*. Remember the Sikh who wouldn't change his turban for a crash helmet? During the 1971 census when all the people in the community were counted, some objected to answering questions about their ancestry. Should you have to reveal to those in authority details about yourself and your family background?

The main job of the police is to prevent crime rather than catch those who commit offences.

Teenagers from different groups fighting

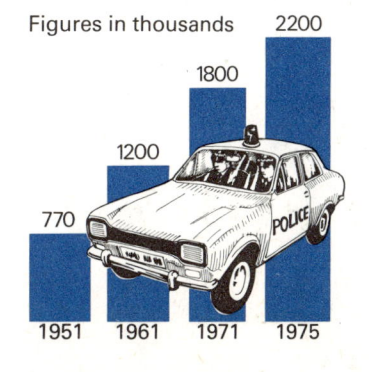

Figures in thousands
770 — 1951
1200 — 1961
1800 — 1971
2200 — 1975

Crime is on the increase

OUR GOVERNMENT AND THE LAW 95

Mounted police

Two constables on the beat – how do they communicate with their station?

A CID officer examining fingerprints

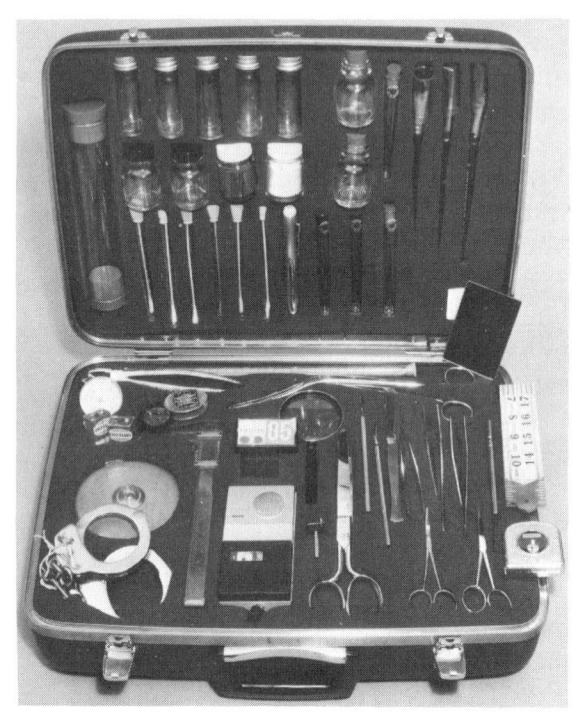

The murder bag – can you identify any of the equipment?

Different aspects of police work

96 INTRODUCING SOCIAL STUDIES

Police at a murder scene – what are the different officers doing?

River police in action

These photographs show some of the specialised tasks performed by the British police in their attempts to maintain law and order for the good of the national community. Today the British police force includes 5000 women.

Things to do and think about

1. Who is the present:
   (a) Leader of the House of Commons
   (b) Speaker of the House of Commons
   (c) Leader of the Opposition
   (d) Lord Chancellor
   (e) Home Secretary
   (f) Foreign Secretary
   (g) Secretary of State for Education and Science
   (h) Secretary of State for Employment
   (i) Secretary of State for Energy
   (j) Secretary of State for Health and Social Security
   (k) Secretary of State for Industry
   (l) President of the Board of Trade?

2. Use the following figures and make a bar (column) diagram to illustrate the result of the October 1974 General Election:

Labour	319 seats
Conservative	276 seats
Liberal	12 seats
Scottish Nationalists	11 seats
Ulster Unionists	10 seats
Welsh Nationalists	3 seats
Others	4 seats
	635

3. Find out for yourself all you can about the:
   (a) legislative
   (b) executive
   (c) judicial

   aspects of government. How does the Lord Chancellor take part in all three?

4. The word democracy comes from the Greek: *demos* = people, *kratos* = rule. Using the *Shorter Oxford English Dictionary* or a Chambers dictionary find

OUR GOVERNMENT AND THE LAW 97

the meaning and origin of the words:
(a) plutocracy   (d) oligarchy
(b) aristocracy (e) monarchy.
(c) bureaucracy

5 Write a script for a party political broadcast on behalf of one of the main parties. Perhaps you will want to use the medium of television. If so you could introduce the following:
(a) interviews
(b) group discussions
(c) pictures to support your arguments
(d) diagrams (e.g. graphs)
(e) music.
Compare your script with articles from the popular press showing different sides of each argument.

6 List ways in which:
(a) You have to limit your freedom in order not to interfere with other people's freedom
(b) the law interferes with your freedom for the sake of the community.

7 If you were Home Secretary, what new measures would you introduce to cut down:
(a) mugging   (d) hijacking
(b) drunken driving (e) kidnapping?
(c) vandalism

8 What points are suggested to you by the following diagram illustrating prison sentences?

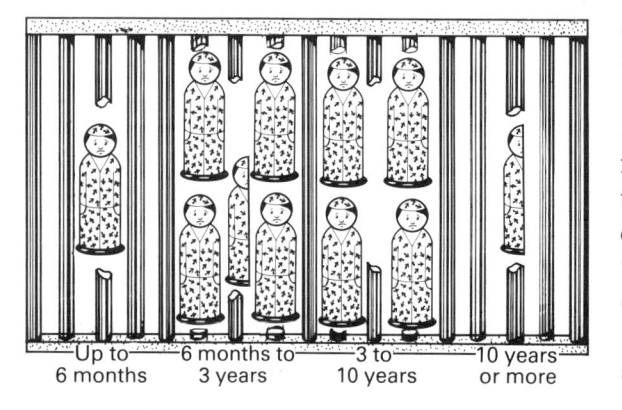

Up to 6 months — 6 months to 3 years — 3 to 10 years — 10 years or more

9 Find out which of the following traffic offences involve the endorsement of a driving licence:
(a) carrying a passenger on your cycle
(b) not stopping after an accident
(c) driving a motor vehicle whilst disqualified
(d) riding a cycle on the footpath
(e) failing to obey a traffic signal.

10 Find out in what ways the British police force differs from that in South Africa and the United States of America.

TOPIC 6.3 **The national economy**

The national economy is concerned with the supply of goods and services to the community. The basic idea of economics is that there is a scarcity of goods and services. No matter how things are organised there will never be enough to go round. There are limited amounts of oil and gas in the North Sea and coal under the ground. There is a scarcity of the basic necessities such as food, clothing, shelter, warmth and of the luxury goods like cars, houses, telephones and TV sets.

Human beings have unlimited wants so there will always be scarcity but there are ways in which we can produce more goods and services. Economists refer to this as *economic growth* or increasing our national output.

We have seen that one way of increasing the amount we produce as a nation is to use the division of labour. Workers are able to specialise because we can exchange our goods and services. In a non-industrial economy the fisherman could swap his surplus fish with the farmer's surplus corn. In an industrial economy workers exchange their labour for wages in the form of money and then exchange the money for goods and services. Labour is treated as a commodity to be bought and sold like everything else. The existence of scarcity means that exchange creates value and each commodity and service has a *price*.

The division of labour or specialisation makes it possible for complicated machinery to be used in manufacturing. Each task is separated and performed by a different person. Henry Ford was one of the first businessmen to use the *conveyor-belt* system. As articles, in the course of production, were conveyed past the workers, each man performed some small task; each of these minor jobs was essential for the production of Ford cars. The Ford Motor Company was founded in 1903 and by the time it stopped producing the famous Ford Model T in 1927, over 15 million had been manufactured and the family car had replaced the family horse.

Machinery is expensive. It can only be used on a large scale if a firm is able to borrow money because people are willing to lend money to it. This money is known to the economist as *investment* in the firm. Such a firm is the Imperial Chemical Industries (ICI). It is one of the largest firms in Britain.

In 1976 ICI raised about £200 million from its shareholders; these are the people who lend money to the company by buying its shares on the Stock Exchange.

The Stock Exchange is the market where stocks and shares are bought and sold. Those who buy stock receive a fixed *interest* on their investment, e.g. if they buy £100 worth at 8 per cent they will receive £8 interest per year. Shareholders hope to receive a *dividend* depending upon the profit made by the company. If the company makes a loss the ordinary shareholder will receive nothing.

The people you can see in the picture are specialists. There is a division of labour between those who are called *brokers* and those known as *jobbers*. The stockbroker buys and sells shares on behalf of his clients, while the jobber buys and sells shares on his own behalf. Jobbers specialise in certain types of

A model T Ford

Spinning cakes of yarn at one of the ICI group's factories in Gloucester

The trading floor of the Stock Exchange – what kind of information is given on the stands?

shares such as shipping, oil, aircraft, insurance or breweries. You will see them clustered round the stands in the picture. The broker makes his way to the right part of the exchange and finds the jobber who is offering the shares he wants at the most favourable price. The broker tries to get the best deal for his client. There are only about $2\frac{1}{4}$ million people who invest through the Stock Exchange but there are many more who invest indirectly. If you pay regular contributions to a life insurance, trade union or pension scheme, or if you put your money into a bank account, the insurance companies and banks invest the money in stocks and shares.

We have had a close look at the working of the Stock Exchange because it is one of the most important economic organisations in the country. Britain's national economy is a *mixed economy* – the means of production are owned partly by private people such as investors and partly by the state on behalf of the whole community. Economists talk about the *private sector* and the *public sector* of the economy. About three quarters of production is carried out by the private sector, hence the importance of the Stock Exchange. The other quarter is run by government-appointed boards, such as the National Coal Board, the Post Office Board and the Railways Board, in which the government invests capital. This money comes from taxation.

Industries run by the government include the basic means of production upon which other industries depend. In the last thirty years about ten large industries have been wholly or partly *nationalised*:

industry	*authority*
Aircraft	British Aerospace
Central Bank	Bank of England Court
Civil Aviation	British Airways
Coal	National Coal Board
Electricity	Electricity Council
Gas	Gas Corporation
Oil	British National Oil Corporation
Post Office	Post Office Board
Railways	British Railways Board
Shipbuilding	British Shipbuilders
Steel	British Steel Corporation

The government supplies many services (such as health, education and defence) with the money it takes from its citizens in the form of *taxes*. There is an interdependence within the national economy. The private and public sectors rely upon each other. For example, private industry uses road, rail and air services, the post office, telephone and electricity, and without them could not operate. In turn those services depend on the revenue received from private industry in the form of payment of telephone and electricity bills, road tax and postage.

Goods are produced by both the public and private sectors – this is called *production*. Production covers both goods and services. The public sector produces mainly services like education, health and transport, for which we sometimes pay directly and sometimes indirectly in the form of taxes. Often we pay both ways. Goods, like bicycles, televisions, food and clothes, are produced mainly by the private sector.

These goods and services reach people through *distribution*. Food is distributed to people through small shops, supermarkets and, more recently in this country, hypermarkets. Consumers can buy their goods in bulk at hypermarkets, often cheaper than in the smaller shops. The health service is often distributed to the people through health clinics – in hospitals and the community – through dentists, specialised services for the old and the handicapped, and through schools, etc.

Another modern development is the buying of goods on *credit* whereby the purchaser can have the goods now and pay later. The extended use of credit cards and hire purchase means that we are moving more towards a credit society.

The British economy is increasingly dependent upon foreign trade. Our imports and exports are now valued at a combined total of over £50 000 million a year. We have to sell goods overseas in order to live. We export manufactured goods such as cars, aircraft, railway locomotives, radio equipment, etc. so that we can import food, raw materials and a number of manufactured goods. Did you know that more than 50 per cent of our food comes from abroad? We import about 80 per cent of our wheat, 60 per cent of our meat and nearly all our beverages such as tea, coffee and cocoa. You will see from the picture that a port such as Southampton is a very busy place.

How are the workers getting on in the modern British economy? Those who still work on the conveyor belt system are frequently bored with their work. It is often monotonous and repetitive. Many workers:

Go to work
To get the cash
To buy the food
To get the strength
To go to work....

The sociologist, Karl Marx, drew attention to the fact that these workers do not feel involved in their work. He called it *alienation*.

The increased use of mechanisation and division of labour has meant that many workers spend all day sitting at a machine, doing one simple task. Many clerical jobs are also dull. The workers become extremely bored, and often the only consolation is the company of other people doing the same thing. But sometimes the machines are so noisy people cannot talk anyway. Some workers see the hours spent at work simply as a means to earn money to spend in their leisure time. Others think job satisfaction is

Unloading fruit at Southampton – what other imports come through these docks?

Workers picketing the factory gates

THE NATIONAL ECONOMY 101

The control room of a power station – automation has made it possible for one man to do many complex jobs

important. Do you? This boredom at work is sometimes the reason why workers strike. For what other reasons do workers go on strike? If a worker does not join his workmates in a strike he is sometimes labelled a scab or blackleg.

One way of improving *industrial relations* is to replace dull, soulless jobs by computers and *automation*, whereby robot machinery performs boring tasks. This would reduce the number of people who would have to do these boring jobs but some would still be needed to tend the machines. One advantage of such mechanisation would be shorter working hours.

The trade unions are naturally suspicious of automation because it means a loss of jobs. See if you can find out the number of workers employed on the railways and down the mines today compared with twenty-five years ago.

Things to do and think about

1. List the main stages in the production of an article made at a factory in your neighbourhood.
2. What are the advantages and disadvantages of:
    (a) division of labour
    (b) automation?
3. Prepare a talk to start a vigorous discussion on *one* of the following:
    (a) The government should take over the twenty-five largest private firms.
    (b) There should be no more nationalisation.
4. In which of these large towns would you expect to find stock exchanges:
    (a) Bonn   (d) Rome
    (b) Moscow   (e) Tokyo?
    (c) Peking

5 Carry out a survey among relatives and friends about their job satisfaction. See if you can find reasons for alienation.
6 Do some research in your local library to find out about:
 (a) The South Sea Bubble of 1720
 (b) The Wall Street Crash of 1929
 (c) The Stock Exchange motto of *Dictum Meum Pactum*
 (d) The Financial Times Index
 (e) The General Strike of 1926.
7 Collect press cuttings to illustrate examples of:
 (a) industrial conflict
 (b) industrial cooperation.
8 Pair the trade union names and types.

name of union	type of union
Association of Scientific, Technical and Managerial Staffs	Industrial
	Craft
	General
	White-collar
National Union of Miners	
Woodworkers' Union	
Transport and General Workers' Union	

9 By observing signs and nameplates used by firms, make a survey of your local town listing:
 (a) ten limited companies (what does 'limited' means, in this sense?)
 (b) what each of these companies makes or sells.
10 List five very different occupations and find out their average rates of pay. Why do you think they attract differing wages or salaries?

Terms used in Unit 6

characteristics	price
immigrants	conveyor belt
New Commonwealth	investment
ethnic	interest
integrate	dividend
racial tension	brokers
freedom	jobbers
government	mixed economy
symbol	private sector
Opposition	public sector
democracy	nationalised
secret ballot	taxes
constituencies	production
common law	distribution
case law	credit
courts	alienation
perjury	industrial relations
anarchy	automation
principle	
economic growth	

THE NATIONAL ECONOMY 103

UNIT 7
Living in the international community

TOPIC 7.1 A divided world

Although we are all members of the human race, we live in a very divided world. There are differences in heredity, environment, culture, traditions, values, religion, politics, race, social conditions. There is no one cause of our differences: the concept of causality means there is no single reason. Differences exist between black and white; between those who live in town and countryside; between rich and poor. One of the things dividing the world is the different systems of government and the different economic systems.

Britain and most other countries of the western world have democratic governments, and forms of capitalism with private ownership of most of the productive units in the economy. The People's Republic of China, the Soviet Union, and many countries mostly situated near these large powers, believe in *communism*; the means of production being owned by the state. In between there is a Third World of *developing countries* which includes some of the worst poverty. A large number of the people in these countries are

Small children and the elderly are the most frequent victims of starvation

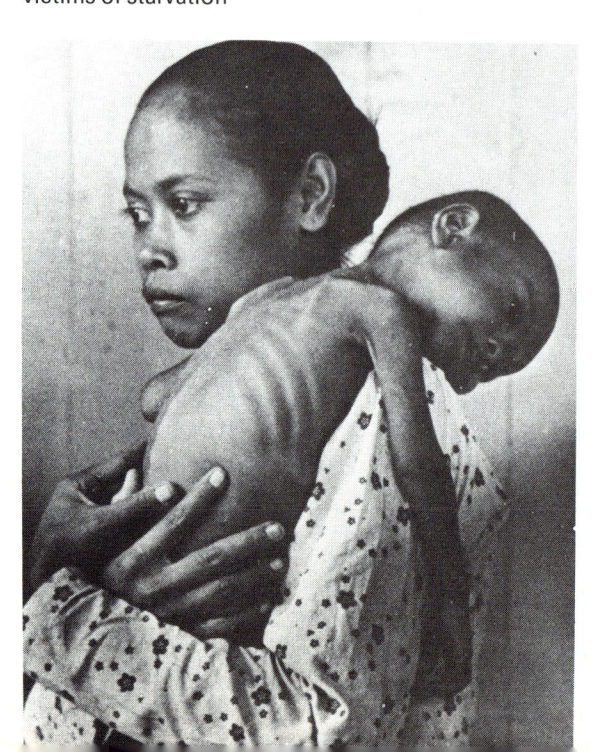

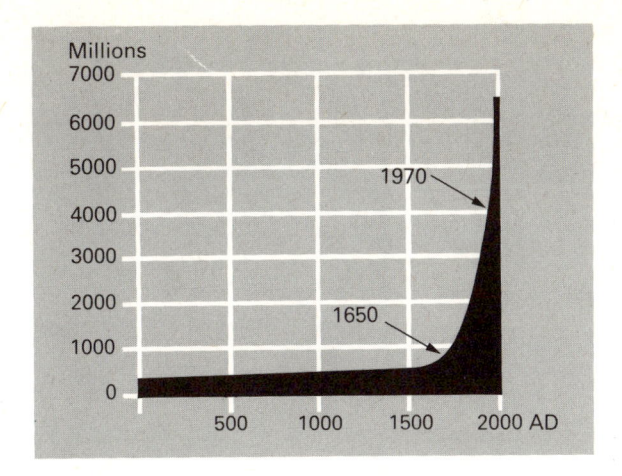

The population explosion

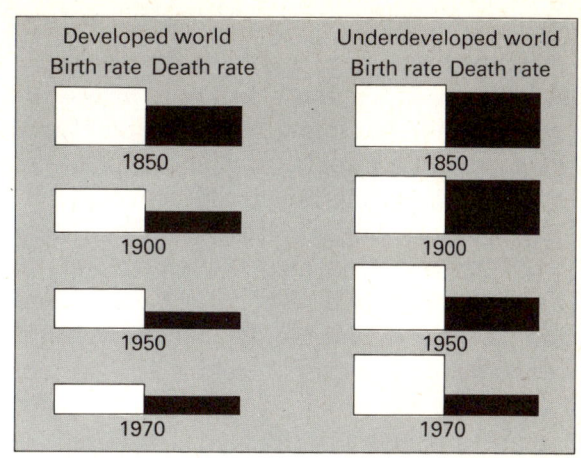

In underdeveloped countries the birth rate is much higher than the death rate

suffering from starvation and sickness. In Bangladesh 40 per cent of the children die before they reach the age of five. Why are they so badly off?

One of the causes of such terrible poverty and misery is the huge growth in the number of people. It has all happened so quickly that we call it the *population explosion*.

Enormous increases in the population began in Britain and other western European countries in the seventeenth and eighteenth centuries. The population grew rapidly as great advances were made in farming, industry and medicine. Such momentous changes took place that historians talk of the Agricultural, Industrial and Medical Revolutions. Food was produced in greater quantities and varieties, following pioneering work in Britain in the eighteenth century: Jethro Tull invented the seed-drill so plants could be sown in rows and kept free from weeds; 'Turnip' Townshend used the four-course rotation of crops; Robert Bakewell reared better breeds of animals while Farmer Coke transformed his barren Norfolk estates into rich and productive land. New industries developed to supply chemicals for fertilisers. Crockery, cutlery, soap and washable clothes allowed people to keep cleaner and fitter. The general health of the people was further improved by such discoveries in medicine as anaesthetic by Morton and Simpson, the antiseptic spray by Lister and a knowledge of germs by a Frenchman called Louis Pasteur. Try to find out more about Pasteur's treatment of rabies, a disease which still has frightening consequences in many parts of the world.

In the eighteenth century the *infant mortality rate* (i.e. the number of children who died before they reached their first birthday) was about 250 per 1000. That is nearly as high as in Bangladesh today. The expectation of life, in eighteenth-century Britain, was less than forty years. Some people lived longer than the average but a look at the old tombstones in a churchyard reveals that many people died very young.

In the poorer countries the changes which we experienced over two centuries are being telescoped into a few years. In 1948 the expectation of life at birth in Sri Lanka was about forty-five, but by 1978 it was approaching seventy. Such countries are overcrowded and a large proportion of the people are very young. Interviewed by the BBC on

A DIVIDED WORLD 105

World Children's Day in June 1976, a British schoolboy remarked that most of the people in Bangladesh are 'kids'. How right he was. In spite of the high infant mortality rate more than half of the population is under the age of nineteen. Bangladesh is in the Third World. Where are the other Third World countries? They are not all in one continent. Can you find Africa, South-east Asia, Central and South America and the Caribbean countries in an atlas or on a map?

In most Third World countries the birth rate is very high but the food supply is very low. They suffer from infertile land, over-farming, *soil erosion* (of large areas where it was once possible to grow food), pests, ignorance of farming methods, excessively heavy rainfall in some places and drought in others. About one-ninth of the earth consists of arid areas which man is turning into desert by inefficient farming methods.

They also suffer the after-effects of colonialisation and imperialism by which the capitalist countries of the western world invaded and controlled other countries taking land, people (as slaves) and raw materials away. Today the effects are still felt through *neo-colonialism*, which drains profit away from the Third World countries to big multi-national companies based in the western world and in Japan.

Look at the cattle in the picture. Can you see their ribs? Are we as a nation doing enough to pay back to the Third World for what we took out under colonialism? Are we giving enough economic aid?

About one person in five, or 800 million of the world's 4000 million people, lives on the verge of starvation. Every year about 35 million die of famine. That is a larger number than the population of Spain. The problem could be lessened by controlling the growth in the world population by *birth control* methods or what is sometimes called *family planning*.

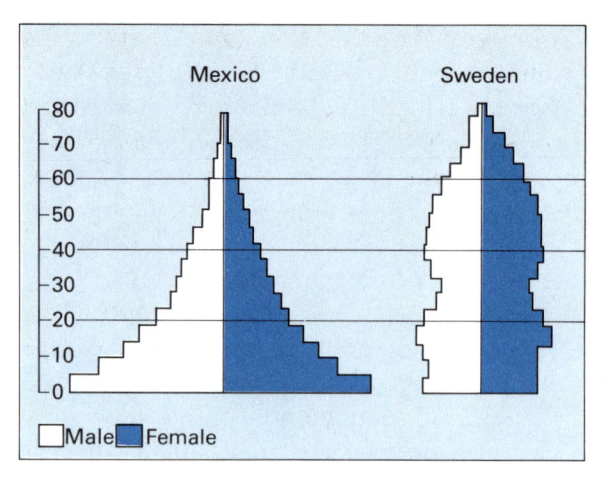

What conclusions can you draw from these population structures of Mexico and Sweden?

The poor land of much of the Third World is unable to support the cattle needed for food

These pills help people to control the size of their families

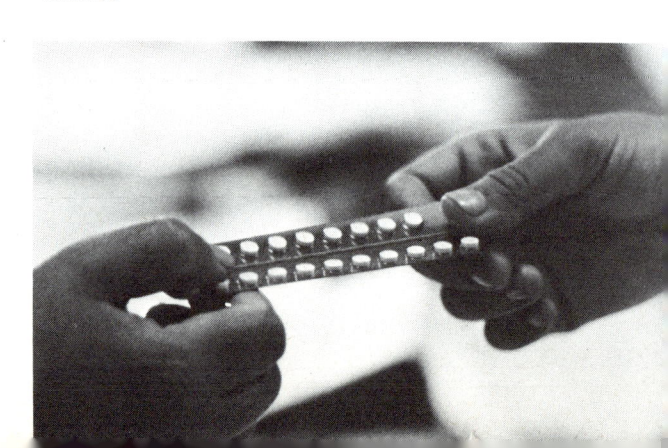

The pills in the picture are contraceptive pills which are very effective if taken regularly. They are issued free to many women in the poorer countries by the World Health Organisation (WHO), a United Nations Agency which we will turn to again in the last topic of this book.

However, family planning only touches the surface of the problem. The poor people of the Third World need lots of children in the hope that some of them will survive to work and help the family and, because of this, the family planning solution is not successful. At present the world population continues to grow and it has been estimated that there may be 15 000 million of us during your lifetime. That is within another fifty years. Imagine four times the number of people living on this earth. We cannot properly feed those who are here. No wonder it is a divided world.

What is needed is a solution to the basic problem of unequal distribution of the world's resources. We cannot rid the world of scarcity but the world's goods can be shared in a fairer way. It may mean that we will have less for ourselves. Do you think this would be a sensible thing?

Can you think of any reasons, apart from selfish ones, why we should not give more than we do in *foreign aid*? How do you think foreign aid should be given? Money spent on training people to make the most of the resources they have, e.g. improved agricultural methods, has a more long-term effect than money spent on food. But food is necessary now for the starving people, President Kennedy once warned the American people that if they did not give enough food away the poorer countries would come and try to take it. Others have said that if the rich send food parcels to the poor they will merely have larger families and the population problem will get worse. Is this just an excuse for not helping? At the moment we do not manage to send them even one per cent of our total national income; that is the target which

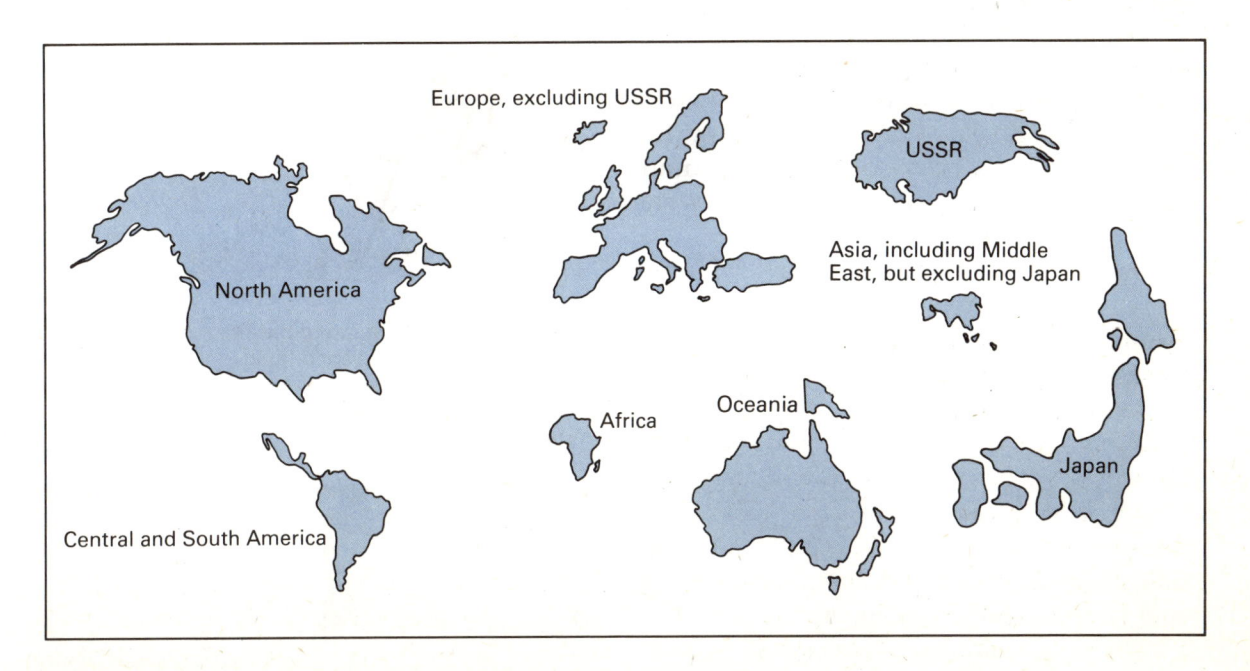

This distorted map shows each of the world's major regions in size according to its wealth

A DIVIDED WORLD 107

New strains of rice are being developed and the people taught better ways of farming to help them feed themselves

the United Nations has set for the rich or *affluent nations*. Should there be more help on an international basis?

The picture shows people in Thailand who have been taught by the Food and Agriculture Organisation to grow better-quality rice. A *green revolution* is taking place with improved strains of rice and wheat. In his book *Reaping the Green Revolution* (Orbis Books, 1975) Dr Sen suggests that the *economic take-off* point, when developing countries advance towards industrial change, can only take place when priority is given to food production.

The Population Countdown Movement have recommended that parents adopt the slogan 'Two will do'. The long-term solution to the population explosion is to educate people so they realise the necessity of having smaller families, and to create the social and economic environment in the poorer parts of the world to make this possible.

The population explosion has been accompanied by a far larger proportion of people

This Indian family living in Dacca have no home – they are typical of thousands

living in towns. The differences between the lifestyle of town-dwellers and rural-dwellers in the poorer countries provide another example of our divided world. Michael Lipton in *Why Poor People Stay Poor: Urban Bias in World Development* (Temple Smith, 1976) has written that:

> The most important class conflict in the poor countries is not between labour and capital. Nor is it between foreign and national interests. It is between the rural classes and the urban classes. The rural sector contains most of the poverty....

Some of you might like to challenge this idea. There is terrible poverty in the increasing number of large towns.

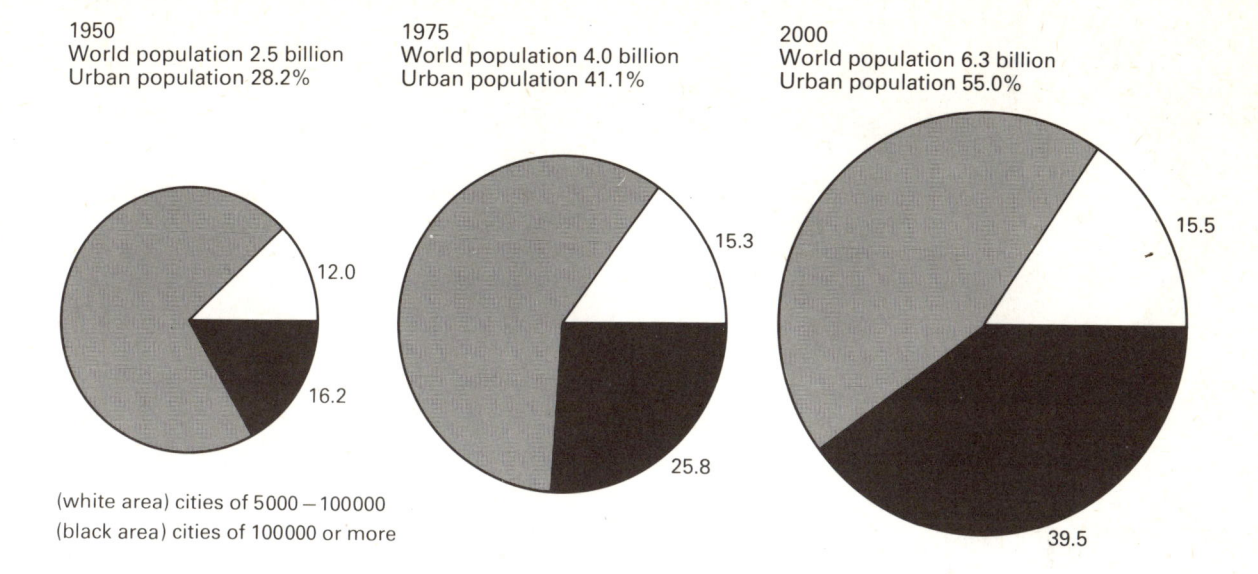

1950
World population 2.5 billion
Urban population 28.2%

1975
World population 4.0 billion
Urban population 41.1%

2000
World population 6.3 billion
Urban population 55.0%

12.0

16.2

15.3

25.8

15.5

39.5

(white area) cities of 5000 – 100000
(black area) cities of 100000 or more

The population explosion has been accompanied by far more people living in towns

Large towns act as magnets and attract people towards them. Every week over one hundred Colombian families move into the capital, Bogota. This kind of thing is happening all over the world. Few *migrant families* move into newly planned towns but rather into places which are unable to cope with them. Even where a new town is built, such as Brazilia, the new capital of Brazil, it may be surrounded by large clusters of hovels where whole families live in makeshift 'homes' made from petrol tins, drainpipes and the like. Many old towns in the poorer countries have few modern facilities. Bogota has changed little since the Spaniards built the narrow streets three centuries ago. The children shown in the photograph can play only in the road.

It was accepted at the United Nations Habitat Conference held in Canada in 1976, that by 1985 there will probably be more than 250 cities with over a million inhabitants. In 1970 there were already 162 places of this size.

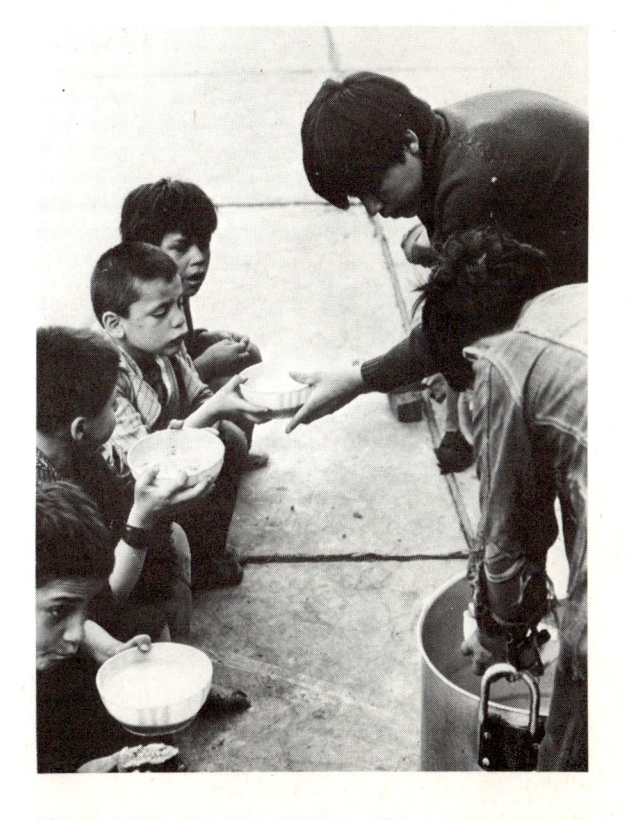

Many children in Third World cities are abandoned because their parents cannot afford to keep them

A DIVIDED WORLD 109

United Nations Habitat symbol – the world, shelter and man

By AD 2000 the typical million-plus city is likely to be in a less developed country. The millions of refugees add to the urban problem because most of them wish to live in towns.

Refugee Blues

Say this city has ten million souls,
Some are living in mansions, some are living in holes:
Yet there's no place for us, my dear, yet there's no place for us.

Once we had a country and we thought it fair,
Look in the atlas and you'll find it there:
We cannot go there now, my dear, we cannot go there now.

In the village churchyard there grows an old yew,
Every spring it blossoms anew:
Old passports can't do that, my dear, old passports can't do that.

The consul banged the table and said,
'If you've got no passport you're officially dead':
But we are still alive, my dear, but we are still alive.

Went to a committee; they offered me a chair;
Asked me politely to return next year:
But where shall we go today, my dear, but where shall we go today?

Came to a public meeting; the speaker got up and said:
'If we let them in they will steal our daily bread;'
He was talking of you and me my dear, he was talking of you and me.

. . .

Saw a poodle in a jacket, fastened with a pin,
Saw a door opened and a cat let in:
But they weren't German Jews, my dear, but they weren't German Jews.

Went down the harbour and stood upon the quay,
Saw the fish swimming as if they were free:
Only ten feet away, my dear, only ten feet away.

Walked through a wood, saw the birds in the trees;
They had no politicians, and sang at their ease:
They weren't the human race, my dear, they weren't the human race.

Dreamed I saw a building with a thousand floors,
A thousand windows and a thousand doors;
Not one of them was ours, my dear, not one of them was ours.

Stood on a great plain in the falling snow;
Ten thousand soldiers marched to and fro:
Looking for you and me, my dear, looking for you and me.

W. H. AUDEN

Things to do and think about

1 Use the following figures to draw a graph illustrating the world population explosion:

year	million
1650	550
1750	750
1800	900
1850	1200
1900	1600
1950	2500
1980	4000
2000	6500

2 List 'killer' diseases of the past which are nearly or completely wiped out in most

parts of the world today. Choose three and explain how these diseases have been tackled. What are the killer diseases of today?

3 Prepare a controversial talk on *one* of these topics:
(a) The simple life is the good life.
(b) Is all economic growth a good thing?
(c) Man should concentrate on the problems of the earth and stop spending money on space travel (or vice versa).

4 How often, in the overflowing streets,
Have I gone forward with the crowd and said
Unto myself, 'The face of every one
That passes by me is a mystery!'
(a) Jot down some thoughts which these words of William Wordsworth bring to your mind.
(b) In what ways can people be lonely in a gigantic crowded city?

5 Collect newspaper cuttings about refugees, for example in:
(a) Eastern Europe
(b) Israel
(c) Arab countries
(d) Africa, south of the Equator.

6 Describe or illustrate the differences between life in:
(a) the capitalist world
(b) the communist world
(c) the Third World.

7 Try to find out what is meant by these expressions:
(a) the Cold War
(b) the Iron Curtain
(c) the Bamboo Curtain
(d) the Red Peril
(e) the Yellow Peril
(f) American imperialism
(g) capitalist colonialism
(h) Black Power
(i) Apartheid
(j) détente.

8 What things could your family most easily give up to make for a fairer distribution of the world's goods?

9 Do you think the existence of the European Economic Community will lead to a *more* or *less* divided world? Give reasons.

TOPIC 7.2 Towards a united world

What hope is there for peace in a world so full of injustices? Are the conflicts in ideas between the *super-powers* of America, Russia and China likely to bring about a nuclear war and the end of civilisation?

The great hope must lie in cooperation and a recognition of how much all the peoples of the world need each other, i.e. our interdependence. With all our differences, human beings find it difficult to give up their *nationalism* and pride in their own national community. Will there ever be a world government?

In some measure, the task has already been started by the *United Nations Organisation*. UNO began in 1945 when delegates of fifty-one nations met in San Francisco and drew up the United Nations Charter. Our picture shows the Earl of Halifax, British Ambassador to the United States, signing the Charter on behalf of Britain.

The terrible destruction man has caused and has weapons to cause again – Hiroshima 1945

There are four main points of the Charter:
1. to maintain peace and security
2. to develop friendly relations among nations
3. to achieve cooperation in solving world problems
4. to be a centre for harmonising the actions of nations in achieving these ends.

For many years after the Second World War, the work of the United Nations was hindered because the People's Republic of China was not allowed to join. China was represented by the government which had ruled China at the end of the war, but after a revolution in 1949 a communist government took over. After many years of arguments, the United Nations accepted Communist China as a full member, which gives the world more hope because this government represents 800 million people, the largest population of any country on earth. It is customary now, if a country has a new government, for it to be quickly recognised by the United Nations even if it takes over after a war or revolution. This happened in the African state of Angola in 1976.

No doubt you noted that the first point of the United Nations Charter was to maintain peace and security. Keeping the peace throughout the world has been of tremendous importance since atomic bombs were dropped by the USA on the Japanese cities of Hiroshima and Nagasaki in August 1945, in

112 INTRODUCING SOCIAL STUDIES

order to bring the Second World War to an end.

We now have the means of destroying our species and all living things upon the earth. Our generation has a great responsibility to work for peace. No other generation has borne such a burden, nor has it had such an incentive to strive for goodwill and understanding among all peoples. Even if the present stock of nuclear bombs is destroyed, the knowledge of how to make them will always be with us. Nuclear energy is one of those things which can be used for good or evil. It can give us gigantic new supplies of power and energy, but it can be misused. The people in the photograph protested in 1975 against the building of any more nuclear power stations in Britain. Notice the banner in the shape of a dustbin representing dangerous nuclear waste material. The protesters delivered a petition to No. 10 Downing Street and also carried a mock plutonium cube, about the size of an Oxo cube, sufficient to wipe out the entire population of the United Kingdom.

While the world remains divided there is always the chance that nuclear bombs may fall into the wrong hands. Fortunately the countries possessing nuclear bombs (the *nuclear powers*) have not acted irresponsibly. There have been military conflicts during the last thirty years but no nuclear wars. There have been so-called *conventional wars* with tanks, aircraft and guns; these are bad enough but nowhere near so terrible as a nuclear war would be. Is it worth destroying civilisation for any '-ism', be it nationalism or patriotism, socialism or communism, capitalism or fascism? You must try to think out this terrible dilemma for yourself. Somebody has suggested that the only way God could make man realise the folly of war was to give him a weapon so terrible that war was no longer worthwhile. Do you think this is a cranky or clever idea? Talk about it among yourselves.

Are demonstrations like this one an effective way to persuade people of the dangers of nuclear power?

The key to such problems lies in who wields the power and authority. Are there some rulers to whom you would not trust nuclear bombs? Whose finger should be on the button?

Do you think national communities should give up the right to govern themselves and allow the United Nations, or some similar body, to exercise the power?

The United Nations organisation is governed by five main principles.

1   All members are sovereign and equal.
2   All members are pledged to solve international disputes by peaceful means.
3   No member shall use force or threaten to use force against the independence of any country.

TOWARDS A UNITED WORLD

An invading army moves out to let in the UN peace-keeping forces

4 All members pledge themselves to assist actions taken in accordance with the UN Charter.
5 The United Nations shall not interfere in the domestic affairs of any country except to enforce world peace.

The principles are sound enough, but unfortunately not all the 137 members carry them out. Threats of force are made and disputes are not always solved by peaceful means. So the United Nations steps in with its peace-keeping forces.

The United Nations is organised with six main governing sections or *UN organs*. The General Assembly is a world parliament including all member countries, each having one vote; it can make recommendations about any matter related to the charter, but it has little real power. The Security Council deals with conflicts which threaten world peace; it has fifteen members, five of whom are permanent members (UK, USA, France, Russia and China). The Secretary General is the most important UN official. The fifteen judges of the International Court of Justice give judgements upon differences or conflicts between countries. The Economic and Social Council encourages cooperation in a very large number of matters including housing conditions, trade, transport, family planning and even crime prevention. The Trusteeship Council has the difficult job of seeing that countries such as South Africa look after their trust territories properly; these territories were allocated to certain governments after the world wars.

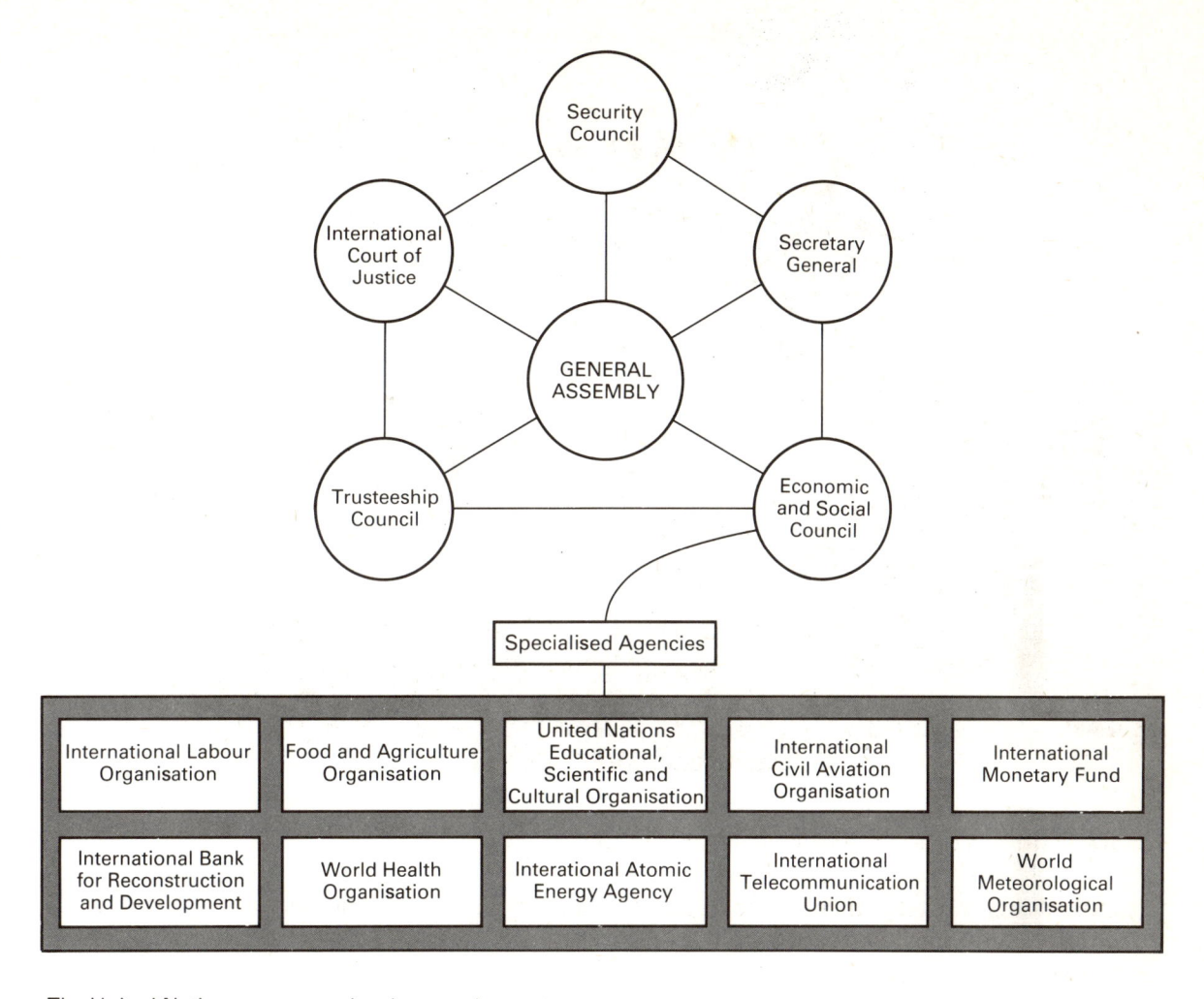

The United Nations organs and main agencies

Finally, there are many UN agencies which are working to transform our divided world into a united one. Their titles usually speak for themselves. Through the Food and Agriculture Organisation (FAO) attempts are made to feed the growing population. The World Health Organisation (WHO) fights diseases such as smallpox and malaria. The World Bank lends money to the poorer countries. The International Labour Organisation is concerned with the world's workers. UNESCO encourages educational, scientific and cultural advances. They all provide examples of cooperating to create a united world in which people can live in peace and with justice.

Things to do and find out

1 Find out about the latest work of one of the following UN agencies:
 (a) International Civil Aviation Organisation
 (b) International Monetary Fund

TOWARDS A UNITED WORLD 115

(c) International Bank for Reconstruction and Development (The World Bank)
(d) International Labour Organisation
(e) International Atomic Energy Authority
(f) International Development Association.

2. Do some research in your library on:
   (a) the Nuclear Test Ban Treaty of 1963
   (b) the Non-Proliferation Treaty of 1968.

3. Find out about the work of your nearest United Nations Association.

4. Is your school a member of the Council for Education in World Citizenship? What is the main purpose of the CEWC?

5. Two of the more recent spheres of UN work are performed by UNDRO and UNEP.
   (a) What do the letters stand for?
   (b) Collect newspaper cuttings to illustrate UN aid:
      (i) to help disaster areas
      (ii) to improve the environment.

6. Draw a strip cartoon to illustrate the work of UNICEF on behalf of the world's children. Some of the work has been concerned with:
   (a) helping refugees
   (b) feeding the hungry
   (c) instructing young people
   (d) community centres
   (e) health centres
   (f) youth clubs.

7. What are the meanings of the words ending with 'ism' referred to on page 113?

8. Do some research to find out about the following world trouble-spots and the attempts made to keep the peace:
   (a) Cuba
   (b) Israeli/Arab borders
   (c) Vietnam
   (d) Cyprus.

9. Design a colourful poster to make clear the advice:
   Give a man a fish and you will feed him for a day,
   Teach a man to fish and you will feed him for life.

10. Write a story beginning with the words, 'Luckily I was able to prevent him pressing the button which would have meant the end of the world. . . .'

Terms used in Unit 7

communism
developing countries
population explosion
infant mortality rate
soil erosion
neo-colonialism
birth control
family planning
foreign aid
affluent nations
green revolution
economic take-off
migrant families
super-powers
nationalism
United Nations Organisation
nuclear powers
conventional wars
UN organs

Glossary of key concepts

A number of key concepts are used throughout this book. *Exact* meanings cannot be given to concepts but they do help us to classify knowledge and study in an orderly way. Some useful *working definitions* are given below.

Concepts are used spirally in this book. In other words, certain basic concepts are used over and over again. You will see how these concepts interrelate and how they can be used in different aspects of social studies.

behaviour: the way a person acts or behaves.
cause: events can often be better understood by a study of the reasons why they happened, that is their causes.
change: the way things adapt in response to social and other influences.
community: a group of people who share a common social life.
conflict: disagreements brought about by opposing points of view.
cooperation: people working together for a common purpose.
differences: variations which exist and are both many and natural.
division of labour: the sharing of work whereby people do particular jobs.
environment: a person's surroundings.
group: two or more people linked by a common purpose or interest.
individual: a person or thing distinguished from all others.
modification: a process by which people or things are changed.
scarcity: exists when things are in short supply in relation to the demand for them.
socialisation: the way by which people learn the customs and values of the groups to which they belong.

Bibliography

Fenton, E. *New Social Studies* (Holt, Rinehart & Winston 1968)
Gleeson, D. & Whitty, G. *Developments in Social Studies Teaching* (Open Books 1976)
Lawton, D. & Dufour, B. *New Social Studies: A Handbook for Teachers in Primary, Secondary and Further Education* (Heinemann Educational 1973)
Mathias, P. *Social Studies* (Teachers' edition) (Blandford 1973)
Philip, W. & Priest, R. *Social Science and Social Studies in Secondary Schools* (Longman 1965)
Schools Council History, Geography and Social Science Project 8-13 *Curriculum Planning* (Collins/ESL 1976)
Schools Council Social Education: *An Experiment in Four Secondary Schools* (Methuen Education/Evans 1974)
Schools Council *Social Studies 8-13* (Methuen Education/Evans 1971)
Taba, H. *Teacher's Handbook to Elementary Social Studies* (Addison-Wesley Publishing Co. 1971)
Warwick, D. (ed) *Integrated Studies in the Secondary School* (University of London Press 1973)

Index

addict 74
Advisory Centre for Education 61
adolescence 26
    Samoan 31
advertising 66, 69
affluent nations 108
Agricultural Revolution 105
aid, foreign 107
alienation 101
anarchy 95
anthropology 55
atomic bombs 112
authority 44, 81, 95, 113
    family 29, 31
    symbol of 91
automation 102

ballot, secret 92
BBC 65
behaviour 13, 40
    emotions 20, 22–3
    instinctive 20
    modified 13
    social 32, 43, 51
Bethnal Green 31, 40
biological drives 23
birth control 106–107
birth rate 79, 106
Board Schools 59
Borneo 31
British Broadcasting Corporation (BBC) 65
Bullock Report (1975) 61
brokers 99

Cameroon 35
causality 17, 38, 104
centres, social 70
change 26, 32
    cultural 52–3, 72
characteristics 88
    physical 15
China, People's Republic of 111, 112
chromosomes 15, 19, 20
classification 7, 44, 80
companionship, human 48
communicating 62–9
communication,
    mass 64
    methods of 52
    non-verbal 62
    road and rail 80–81
communism 104, 113
community 48, 70–78, 100
    international, 104–116

national 88–103, 111
school 23
urban 79
village 70, 72
community life 85
community spirit 70
conflict 8, 19, 38, 44
    and crime 95
    family 31, 32, 36, 40
    of interests 65
    religious 90
    see also role conflict
conformity 8
congestion 81
conservation 76
constituencies 92
contraception 37, 106–107
conurbation 82
conveyor-belt 99
cooperation 25, 54
    kibbutz 31
    learning 54, 57, 59
    political 88, 111
    at work 37, 72
    UN agencies 115
counties, metropolitan 82
countries, developing 104
country-dwellers 73
Courts 93
    Crown 94
    Magistrates' 93
credit (money) 100–101
cultural change 52–3, 72
culture 51
    Hadza 51, 52–3
    Muslim 90
customs 8, 28, 88

decisions 22, 45
democracy 92, 97
development, social 43
differences 7, 15–19, 55, 74, 104
    biological 20
    cultural 51
    social 23, 35, 67
dividend 99
division of labour 37, 70, 72, 98–9, 101
divorce 36

economics 55, 98
economy,
    growth (economic) 98
    national 98–103
    mixed 100
    take-off (economic) 108
education 23, 51–69
    basic 52
    co-education 62
    formal 53, 56–62
    informal 20, 36, 52, 53
environment 16, 20, 51
    education and 59
    factors (environmental) 39–40

heredity and 23, 43
    home 57
    influences of 18, 36
    modification 73
emotions 20
    behaviour and 22
equality of opportunity 54
ethics 55
evidence 59, 94
evolution 20
exchange 52, 71
expansion schemes 84
experimental activity (in school) 59

family 28–42
    abolition of 25, 35
    child-centred 34
    conflicts 38–42
    deprived 77
    extended 31
    and friends 29, 45
    functions 36–8
    human 19
    migrant 109
    nuclear 30, 31
    planning 37, 106–107
    relationships 31–2, 44
    size 30–31, 107, 108
    television and 64
fantasies 11–12
Food and Agricultural Organisation (FAO) 108
Ford, Henry 99
foreign aid 107
formal social control 70, 94
freedom 19, 90
friends 29, 43–50
    influence of 8, 47, 59, 74
friendship 47–50
function, natural 36

general election 92
generation gap 44–5, 47, 77
goods, distribution of 110
government 91–8
    local 82
    world 111
green belts 85
green revolution 108
group 44, 88
    activities 26
    family 30–33, 35
    influences 47
    membership 12
    minority 89
    norms 8
    see also peer group; playgroup; pressure group

Hadza 51–2, 55
heredity 15–16, 20
hidden persuaders 66
homo sapiens 20

118   INDEX

House of Commons 63, 91–3
housing 23, 40, 80, 95
hypothesis 11

immigrants 23, 77, 89–90
Independent Broadcasting Authority (IBA), 65
individual 6, 13, 29, 54
   heredity and 15
   identity 7
   influences on 18, 43, 57
   responsibilities 25, 75
industrial relations 102
Industrial Revolution 105
industries 100
industrialisation 53
inequalities 18, 19
infant mortality rate 105
influences 47
instincts 20
integration, 90
intelligence 54
interaction, social 63
interdependence 32, 49, 59, 80–81
interest (money) 99
introvert 49
investment 99

jobber 99

kibbutz 31
knowledge 54

law 91–7
   case 93
   common 93
Leakey, Richard 20
life, expectation of 105
life-cycle 32
lifestyle 47

marriage 35, 36
mass media 66
Mead, Margaret 31, 45
Medical Revolution 105
minorities, ethnic 89
minority interest 65
mobility of labour 73
modification 13, 73
Motilone Indians 7–8
motives 39

National Union of School Students (NUSS) 60
nationalisation 100
nationalism 111
nations, affluent 108
neo-colonialism 106
new commonwealth 89

New Guinea 6, 7
newspapers 66–7
Noise Abatement Society 74
norms 95
   group 8
nuclear powers 113

occupations, traditional 70
Open University 65
opinion, mass 67
opportunities, equal 17, 18
Opposition, the 92
Owen Robert 25

parents 15, 16, 17–18, 28–42
   conflict and 39–40, 43–4
   crime and 95
parliament 92
   regional 23
peer group 44
perjury 94
personality 43
   influences on 47, 57
Piaget, Jean 56
playgroup 57
pollution, 73–7
population 79
   explosion 105
   world 107
Population Countdown Movement 108
prejudices 65, 66, 90
pressure group 26, 79
price 99
principle (conscience) 90, 95
production 100
psychology 55

questionnaire 64

racial tension 90
relations (family) 28–34; see also 35–43
relations, industrial 102
research, social 64
role 12, 14
   adult 45
   conflict 12–13, 14
Russia 35, 111

Samoa 31, 45
sampling 64
scarcity 59, 66, 98, 107
schools 47, 54, 56–62
   community 23
   discipline 57
   nursery 57
Schools Council 60–61
sectors,
   private 100
   public 100

selection, natural 20
Shelter 79–80
shopping precincts 85
skills, traditional 52
slums 40, 79
social control 32
social nucleus 85
social scientists 17
socialisation 28, 29, 33, 36
society 23, 26, 28, 29
   credit 101
   differences in 20
   ideal 25
   industrial 51
   non-industrial 45, 51
   obligations of 18
sociology 55
soil erosion 106
sources (of news) 66
specialisation 70–71, 98, 99
status 32, 35
Stock Exchange 99–100
suburbs 85
super-powers 111
survey 64

taxes 100
teenager 43–5
television 64–5, 67, 69
theory 11, 20
Third World 104–110
town-dwellers 73, 79, 85
towns 40, 79–87, 108, 109
   amenities 72–3
   new 82, 84
   overspill 84
   Third World 108–9, 110
traditions 28, 52, 90, 94
twilight zone 80

uniqueness 6, 15
UNESCO 115
United Nations 107, 111–16
   Charter 111, 112
   Habitat Conference (1976) 109
   Organisation (UNO) 111
   organs 114–16
   Universal Declaration of Human Rights 18–19

values 21, 22
village-dwellers 72

wars, conventional 113
world
   divided 104–111, 113
   united 111–16
World Health Organisation (WHO) 107, 115

Acknowledgements

The author and publisher wish to thank the following who have given permission for the use of copyright material: Advisory Centre for Education for an extract from a publication; George Allen & Unwin (Publishers) Limited for an extract from *Little Johnny's Confession* by Brian Patten; Blandford Press Limited for an extract from *Groups and Communities* by Paul Matthias; Curtis Brown Limited on behalf of Ronald Frankenburg for an extract from *Communities in Britain* and the Estate of John Steinbeck for an extract from *The Pearl*; The Daily Telegraph Limited for two headlines from the *Daily Telegraph*, April 1976; J. M. Dent & Sons Limited for an extract from the poem 'The People Upstairs' by Ogden Nash from *The Book of Verses*; Gerald Duckworth & Company Limited for an extract from *Change in the Village* by George Bourne; *Eastern Evening News* for extracts and headlines; Faber & Faber Limited for extracts from *Lord of the Flies* by William Golding, and the poem 'Refugee Blues' from *Collected Poems* by W. H. Auden (also known as I from the series 'Ten Songs'); David Higham Associates Limited on behalf of Charles Causley for an extract from 'Timothy Winters' from *Collected Poems*; Michael Joseph Limited for an extract from *A Kestrel for a Knave* by Barry Hines; London Express News and Feature Services for extracts from the *Sun* newspaper; Methuen Children's Books Limited for the poem 'The Old Sailor' from *Now We Are Six* by A. A. Milne; John Murray Limited for an extract from *Scott of the Antarctic* by George Seaver; Northern Songs Limited for an extract from the song 'Imagine' by John Lennon © 1971; Oxford University Press for an extract from *The Realm of a Rain Queen* by E. J. & J. D. Krige; Penguin Books Limited for extracts from *The Family and Marriage in Britain* by Ronald Fletcher; *Child Care and Growth* by John Bowlby and *The Penguin Book of Comic and Curious Verse* by J. M. Cohen; Laurence Pollinger Limited on behalf of William Saroyan for an extract from *Little Children* published by Faber & Faber Limited and an extract from *Coming of Age in Samoa* by Margaret Mead; Christine Pomfret for her poem 'Adolescence'; Routledge & Kegan Paul Limited for an extract from *Family and Kinship in East London* by M. Young and P. Willmott; The Royal Town Planning Institute for an extract from an article by David Sibley published in *The Planner*, Volume 62, May 1976; Simon & Schuster Incorporated for an extract from *Baby and Child Care* by Benjamin Spock; The Society of Authors on behalf of the Bernard Shaw Estate for an extract from *Misalliance*; The Times Newspapers Limited for extracts from articles published May and June 1976 and a headline from *The Sunday Times*, April 1976; Teo-Essex Music Limited for an extract from the song 'The Big Rock Candy Mountains' by John & Alan Lomas.

The publishers wish to thank the following for permission to redraw artwork:
New Society, London, the weekly review of the social sciences p. 82; World Bank p. 107; Population Reference Bureau Inc. p. 109 (top).

The author and publisher wish to acknowledge the following photograph sources:
M. Abrahams p. 101 bottom; ATV p. 53 top left; Peter Baker pp. 53 bottom left, 55 bottom; Cyril Bernard p. 55 top middle; British Dental Hygiene Society p. 52; British Railways Board pp. 49, 81 top right; British Transport Docks Board p. 101 middle; Jim Brownbill p. 81 bottom; Camera Press pp. 7, 62, 93, 95, 109; Central Electricity Generating Board p. 102; Central Office of Information pp. 59, 68, 78; Ron Chapman/Sheelah Latham pp. 53 bottom right, 57, 67; Commissioner of Police of the Metropolis pp. 13, 75 bottom, 96, 97; Community Service Volunteer p. 48 bottom; Consumers Association p. 73 right; Daily Mirror p. 65; FAO Photo p. 108 left; Ford Motor Co. p. 99 top; Granada TV p. 41 top left; Henry Grant pp. 44 bottom, 89 right; Greater London Council p. 79 top; Richard & Sally Greenhill p. 53 top right; Health Education Council p. 18 top; Courtesy of HM Postmaster General p. 80 bottom; ICI Fibres Limited p. 99 middle; Kentish Times p. 85; Keystone Press Agency pp. 6, 32, 41 top right, 90 right, 112, 113; London Evening Standard p. 39; Mansell Collection p. 25; Methodist Home Mission p. 29; Methodist Missionary Society p. 106 middle; Milton Keynes Development Corporation p. 84; John S. Morland p. 101 top; Nationwide Building Society p. 30 top right; Michael Neale p. 108 right; News of the World p. 43; Norwich Corporation p. 87; Norfolk County Council pp. 75 top left, 77 middle and bottom; NSPCC p. 17 right; Polaroid (UK) Ltd pp. 15 top left, p. 15 bottom, p. 48 top; RTHPL p. 30 bottom left; Salvation Army Information Services p. 89 top left; Shelter (Nick Hedges) p. 40; Shelter (Stuart McPherson) pp. 50, 79 bottom; The Sun pp. 8, 16 bottom left, 30 top left, 36 top, 64, 75 top right, 94; Sunday Express p. 33; Sunday Mirror p. 36 left; Thames TV pp. 71, 90 left; United Nations pp. 18 bottom, 35 top, 77 top, 111, 114; UNICEF p. 44 top; John Walker & Sons Ltd. p. 35 bottom; C. James Webb p. 15 top right; Janine Wiedel p. 72 top; WHO pp. 17 left, 104, 106 bottom.

The publishers have made every effort to trace the copyright holders, but if they have inadvertently overlooked any, they will be pleased to make the necessary arrangements at the earliest opportunity.